Rainbow Edition

Reading Mastery I
Spelling Book

Siegfried Engelmann • Elaine C. Bruner

Macmillan/McGraw–Hill

Columbus, Ohio

SRA Macmillan/McGraw-Hill
250 Old Wilson Bridge Road
Suite 310
Worthington, Ohio 43085
Printed in the United States of America.
ISBN 0-02-686331-6
1 2 3 4 5 6 7 8 9 0 IPC 99 98 97 96 95 94

Note: *Do not* begin spelling activities with the first reading lesson.

Introduction

There are 111 lessons in the spelling book. Each lesson takes approximately 10 minutes to teach. If you are teaching small groups, present the first spelling lesson after a group completes Lesson 50 in Presentation Book A. If you are teaching the entire class, you may start after the *lowest performing group* reaches Lesson 40 in Presentation Book A. Do not include the spelling lesson as part of the reading period.

The children need the following skills to begin the spelling lessons:

1. identifying and writing the various sounds such as **m, t, s;**
2. "saying the sounds" in a word;
3. "saying a word fast."

Overview of Skills Taught

The spelling program is designed so that the children spell by sounds rather than by letter names. That is, they say the sounds in a word, then write the word.

In the early spelling lessons, the children write single sounds from dictation.

In Spelling Lesson 3, the children begin a more complex sound-writing task. The teacher dictates two sounds, with a pause between them. The children indicate what sound they are going to write first and what sound they are going to write next. Then the children write the sounds.

(Teachers are sometimes concerned that the children will begin pausing between sounds in their reading if pausing is introduced in the spelling. This response does not usually occur. The work with spelling facilitates the children's performance in reading.)

Beginning with Spelling Lesson 5, the children review saying the sounds in regularly spelled words. These words are presented orally.

Beginning with Spelling Lesson 9, the children combine the skills taught in previous lessons. They say the sounds in a word without pausing between the sounds. The teacher demonstrates how to say the sounds the "hard way," which involves saying the sounds with pauses between them. Finally, the children write the word.

At Spelling Lesson 33, the children start spelling words that are slightly irregular, such as **is** and **has.**

At Spelling Lesson 79, the children begin spelling irregular words such as **was** and **arm.**

Then, at Spelling Lesson 82, the children start writing an entire sentence from dictation. The children are responsible for remembering how to spell each of the words the right way.

General Procedures

Give each child lined paper and a pencil. Since each lesson takes only a few lines, you may want to collect the papers and pass them out daily until the page is filled.

It is preferable for children to write the dictated sounds in a row (across) instead of a column (down the paper).

Beginning at Spelling Lesson 5 and continuing through Spelling Lesson 111, a series of words is dictated. The children should write these words in a column (one word below the next).

Depending on the performance of the group you may be able to teach more than one spelling lesson per day and/or skip every fourth lesson. The criterion for accelerating or skipping is that the children make *very few* errors.

Spelling Lesson 1

SOUND WRITING

TASK Children write i and r

a. You're going to write some sounds.
b. Here's the first sound you're going to write. Listen. **iii.**
What sound? (Signal.) *iii.*
c. Write **iii.** Check children's responses.
d. Next sound. Listen. **rrr.** What sound? (Signal.) *rrr.*
e. Write **rrr.** Check children's responses.
f. Next sound. Listen. **rrr.** What sound? (Signal.) *rrr.*
g. Write **rrr.** Check children's responses.
h. Repeat *f* and *g* for the following sounds: **i, r, i.**

END OF SPELLING LESSON

Spelling Lesson 2

SOUND WRITING

TASK Children write r and i

a. You're going to write some sounds.
b. Here's the first sound you're going to write. Listen. **rrr.**
What sound? (Signal.) *rrr.*
c. Write **rrr.** Check children's responses.
d. Next sound. Listen. **iii.** What sound? (Signal.) *iii.*
e. Write **iii.** Check children's responses.
f. Next sound. Listen. **iii.** What sound? (Signal.) *iii.*
g. Write **iii.** Check children's responses.
h. Repeat *f* and *g* for the following sounds: **r, r, i.**

END OF SPELLING LESSON

Spelling Lesson 3

SOUND WRITING

TASK 1 Children write r, a, and i

a. You're going to write some sounds.
b. Here's the first sound you're going to write. Listen. **rrr.**
What sound? (Signal.) *rrr.*
c. Write **rrr.** Check children's responses.
d. Next sound. Listen. **aaa.** What sound? (Signal.) *aaa.*
e. Write **aaa.** Check children's responses.
f. Next sound. Listen. **iii.** What sound? (Signal.) *iii.*
g. Write **iii.** Check children's responses.
h. Repeat *f* and *g* for the sound **a.**

TASK 2 Children write r a

a. Here are the sounds you're going to write next. Listen.
rrr (pause two seconds) **aaa.**
b. Listen again. **rrr** (pause two seconds) **aaa.**
c. Your turn to say the sounds. Get ready. Clap. *rrr.*
(Pause two seconds.) Clap. *aaa.* Repeat until firm.
d. What sound are you going to write first? (Signal.) *rrr.*
e. What sound are you going to write next? (Signal.) *aaa.*
f. Repeat *d* and *e* until firm.
g. Write **rrr** and **aaa.** Check children's responses.

END OF SPELLING LESSON

Spelling Lesson 4

SOUND WRITING

TASK 1 Children write **i**, **a**, and **r**

a. You're going to write some sounds.
b. Here's the first sound you're going to write. Listen. **iii.**
  What sound? (Signal.) *iii.*
c. Write **iii.** Check children's responses.
d. Next sound. Listen. **aaa.** What sound? (Signal.) *aaa.*
e. Write **aaa.** Check children's responses.
f. Next sound. Listen. **rrr.** What sound? (Signal.) *rrr.*
g. Write **rrr.** Check children's responses.
h. Repeat *f* and *g* for the sound **a.**

TASK 2 Children write **r a**

a. Here are the sounds you're going to write next. Listen.
  rrr (pause two seconds) **aaa.**
b. Listen again. **rrr** (pause two seconds) **aaa.**
c. Your turn to say the sounds. Get ready. Clap. *rrr.*
  (Pause two seconds.) Clap. *aaa.* Repeat until firm.
d. What sound are you going to write first? (Signal.) *rrr.*
e. What sound are you going to write next? (Signal.) *aaa.*
f. Repeat *d* and *e* until firm.
g. Write **rrr** and **aaa.** Check children's responses.

END OF SPELLING LESSON

Spelling Lesson 5

SOUND WRITING

TASK 1 Children write **r, i,** and **a**

a. You're going to write some sounds.
b. Here's the first sound you're going to write. Listen. **rrr.**
  What sound? (Signal.) *rrr.*
c. Write **rrr.** Check children's responses.
d. Next sound. Listen. **iii.** What sound? (Signal.) *iii.*
e. Write **iii.** Check children's responses.
f. Repeat *d* and *e* for the sounds **a** and **r.**

TASK 2 Children write **a i**

a. Here are the sounds you're going to write next. Listen.
  aaa (pause two seconds) **iii.**
b. Listen again. **aaa** (pause two seconds) **iii.**
c. Your turn to say the sounds. Get ready. Clap. *aaa.*
  (Pause two seconds.) Clap. *iii.* Repeat until firm.
d. What sound are you going to write first? (Signal.) *aaa.*
e. What sound are you going to write next? (Signal.) *iii.*
f. Repeat *d* and *e* until firm.
g. Write **aaa** and **iii.** Check children's responses.

SAY THE SOUNDS

TASK 3 Children say the sounds in **it, in**

a. Listen. You're going to say the sounds in the word (pause) **it.**
b. What word? (Signal.) *It.* Yes, **it.**
c. Hold up your hand. Saying the sounds in (pause) **it.** Get ready.
  Signal for **i** and **t.** The children say *iiit* without pausing between
  the sounds.
d. Again. Repeat *c* until firm.
e. When **iiit** is firm, say: Say it fast. (Signal.) *It.*
f. Yes, what word? (Signal.) *It.* Good. You said the sounds in
  (pause) **it.**
g. Repeat *a* through *f* for **in.**

END OF SPELLING LESSON

Spelling Lesson 6

SOUND WRITING

TASK 1   Children write **a**, **i**, and **r**

a. You're going to write some sounds.
b. Here's the first sound you're going to write. Listen. **aaa**.
What sound?   (Signal.) *aaa.*
c. Write **aaa**.   Check children's responses.
d. Next sound. Listen. **iii**. What sound?   (Signal.) *iii.*
e. Write **iii**.   Check children's responses.
f. Repeat *d* and *e* for the sounds **r** and **i**.

TASK 2   Children write **a r**

a. Here are the sounds you're going to write next. Listen.
aaa   (pause two seconds) **rrr**.
b. Listen again. **aaa**   (pause two seconds) **rrr**.
c. Your turn to say the sounds. Get ready.   Clap. *aaa.*
(Pause two seconds.) Clap. *rrr.* Repeat until firm.
d. What sound are you going to write first?   (Signal.) *aaa.*
e. What sound are you going to write next?   (Signal.) *rrr.*
f. Repeat *d* and *e* until firm.
g. Write **aaa** and **rrr**.   Check children's responses.

SAY THE SOUNDS

TASK 3   Children say the sounds in **at**, **in**

a. Listen. You're going to say the sounds in the word   (pause) **at**.
b. What word?   (Signal.) *At.* Yes, **at**.
c. Hold up your hand. **Saying the sounds in**   (pause) **at**. Get ready.
Signal for **a** and **t**. The children say *aaat* without pausing between the sounds.
d. Again.   Repeat *c* until firm.
e. When **aaat** is firm, say: **Say it fast.**   (Signal.) *At.*
f. Yes, what word?   (Signal.) *At.* **Good. You said the sounds in**
(pause) **at**.
g. Repeat *a* through *f* for **in**.

Spelling Lesson 7

SOUND WRITING

TASK 1   Children write **t** and **r**

a. You're going to write some sounds.
b. Here's the first sound you're going to write. Listen. **t**.
What sound?   (Signal.) *t.*
c. Write **t**.   Check children's responses.
d. Next sound. Listen **rrr**. What sound?   (Signal.) *rrr.*
e. Write **rrr**.   Check children's responses.

TASK 2   Children write **t a, t i**

a. Here are the sounds you're going to write next. Listen.
t (pause two seconds) **aaa**.
b. Listen again. **t** (pause two seconds) **aaa**.
c. Your turn to say the sounds. Get ready.   Clap. *t.*
(Pause two seconds.) Clap. *aaa.* Repeat until firm.
d. What sound are you going to write first?   (Signal.) *t.*
e. What sound are you going to write next?   (Signal.) *aaa.*
f. Repeat *d* and *e* until firm.
g. Write **t** and **aaa**.   Check children's responses.
h. Repeat *a* through *g* for the sounds **t i**.

SAY THE SOUNDS

TASK 3   Children say the sounds in **it**, **an**

a. Listen. You're going to say the sounds in the word   (pause) **it**.
b. What word?   (Signal.) *It.* Yes, **it**.
c. Hold up your hand. **Saying the sounds in**   (pause) **it**. Get ready.
Signal for **i** and **t**. The children say *iiit* without pausing between the sounds.
d. Again.   Repeat *c* until firm.
e. When **iiit** is firm, say: **Say it fast.**   (Signal.) *It.*
f. Yes, what word?   (Signal.) *It.* **Good. You said the sounds in**
(pause) **it**.
g. Repeat *a* through *f* for **an**.

END OF SPELLING LESSON

Spelling Lesson 8

SOUND WRITING

TASK 1 Children write **t** and **i**

a. You're going to write some sounds.
b. Here's the first sound you're going to write. Listen. **t.**
What sound? (Signal.) *t.*
c. Write **t.** Check children's responses.
d. Next sound. Listen. **iii.** What sound? (Signal.) *iii.*
e. Write **iii.** Check children's responses.

TASK 2 Children write **t r, a t**

a. Here are the sounds you're going to write next. Listen.
t (pause two seconds) **rrr.**
b. Listen again. **t** (pause two seconds) **rrr.**
c. Your turn to say the sounds. Get ready. Clap. *t.*
(Pause two seconds.) Clap. *rrr.* Repeat until firm.
d. What sound are you going to write first? (Signal.) *t.*
e. What sound are you going to write next? (Signal.) *rrr.*
f. Repeat *d* and *e* until firm.
g. Write **t** and **rrr.** Check children's responses.
h. Repeat *a* through *g* for the sounds **a t.**

SAY THE SOUNDS

TASK 3 Children say the sounds in **am, it**

a. Listen. You're going to say the sounds in the word (pause) **am.**
b. What word? (Signal.) *Am.* Yes, **am.**
c. Hold up your hand. Saying the sounds in (pause) **am. Get ready.**
Signal for **a** and **m.** The children say *aaammm* without pausing
between the sounds.
d. Again. Repeat *c* until firm.
e. When **aaammm** is firm, say: Say it fast. (Signal.) *Am.*
f. Yes, what word? (Signal.) *Am* Good. You said the sounds in
(pause) **am.**
g. Repeat *a* through *f* for **it.**

END OF SPELLING LESSON

Spelling Lesson 9

SOUND WRITING

TASK 1 Children write **r i, t a, r t**

a. Here are the sounds you're going to write. Listen.
rrr (pause two seconds) **iii.**
b. Listen again. **rrr** (pause two seconds) **iii.**
c. Your turn to say the sounds. Get ready. Clap. *rrr.*
(Pause two seconds.) Clap. *iii.* Repeat until firm.
d. What sound are you going to write first? (Signal.) *rrr.*
e. What sound are you going to write next? (Signal.) *iii.*
f. Repeat *d* and *e* until firm.
g. Write **rrr** and **iii.** Check children's responses.
h. Repeat *a* through *g* for the sounds **t a.**
i. Repeat *a* through *g* for the sounds **r t.**

SAY THE SOUNDS

TASK 2 Children say the sounds in **an, in**

a. Listen. You're going to say the sounds in the word (pause) **an.**
b. What word? (Signal.) *An.* Yes, **an.**
c. Hold up your hand. Saying the sounds in (pause) **an. Get ready.**
Signal for **a** and **n.** The children say *aaannn* without pausing
between the sounds.
d. Again. Repeat *c* until firm.
e. When **aaannn** is firm, say: Say it fast. (Signal.) *An.*
f. Yes, what word? (Signal.) *An.* Good. You said the sounds in
(pause) **an.**
g. Repeat *a* through *f* for **in.**

WORD WRITING

TASK 3   Children write **it**

a. Everybody, get ready to say the sounds in (pause) **it**. Get ready.
Signal for each sound as the children say *iiit*.

b. Let's do it the hard way. My turn. Saying the sounds in (pause) **it**.
Iii (pause two seconds) **t**. I said the sounds the hard way.

c. Do it with me. Saying the sounds in (pause) **it** the hard way.
Get ready. Signal for each sound as you and the children say **iii**
(pause two seconds) **t**. Repeat until firm.

d. Your turn. All by yourselves. Saying the sounds in (pause) **it**
the hard way. Get ready. Signal for each sound as the children
say *iii* (pause) *t*. The children are to pause between the sounds.
Good.

e. Again. Saying the sounds in (pause) **it** the hard way. Get ready.
Signal for each sound as the children say *iii* (pause) *t*. The
children are to pause two seconds between the sounds.

f. Everybody, write the sounds in (pause) **it**. Check children's
responses. You wrote the word (pause) **it**. What word did you
write? (Signal.) *It.*

END OF SPELLING LESSON

Spelling Lesson 10

SOUND WRITING

TASK 1   Children write **n**

a. You're going to write a sound.

b. Here's the sound you're going to write. Listen. **nnn**.
What sound? (Signal.) *nnn.*

c. Write **nnn**. Check children's responses.

TASK 2   Children write **t r, n t**

a. Here are the sounds you're going to write next. Listen.
t (pause two seconds) **rrr**.

b. Listen again. **t** (pause two seconds) **rrr**.

c. Your turn to say the sounds. Get ready. Clap. *t.*
(Pause two seconds) Clap. *rrr.* Repeat until firm.

d. What sound are you going to write first? (Signal.) *t.*

e. What sound are you going to write next? (Signal.) *rrr.*

f. Repeat *d* and *e* until firm.

g. Write **t** and **rrr**. Check children's responses.

h. Repeat *a* through *g* for the sounds **n t**.

TASK 3   Children write **n a t**

a. Here are some sounds you're going to write next. Listen.
nnn (pause) **aaa** (pause) **t**.

b. Listen again. **nnn** (pause) **aaa** (pause) **t**.

c. Say the sounds with me. Get ready. Clap for each sound as you and
the children say **nnn** (pause) **aaa** (pause) **t**. Repeat until firm.

d. What sound are you going to write first? (Signal.) *nnn.*

e. What sound are you going to write next? (Signal.) *aaa.*

f. What sound are you going to write next? (Signal.) *t.*

g. Repeat *d* through *f* until firm.

h. Write **nnn** (pause) **aaa** (pause) **t**. Check children's responses.

SAY THE SOUNDS

TASK 4   Children say the sounds in **at**, **it**

a. Listen. You're going to say the sounds in the word (pause) **at**.

b. What word? (Signal.) *At.* Yes, **at**.

c. Hold up your hand. Saying the sounds in (pause) **at**. Get ready.
Signal for **a** and **t**. The children say *aaat* without pausing between
the sounds.

d. Again. Repeat *c* until firm.

e. When **aaat** is firm, say: Say it fast. (Signal.) *At.*

f. Yes, what word? (Signal.) *At.* Good. You said the sounds in
(pause) **at**.

g. Repeat *a* through *f* for **it**.

WORD WRITING

TASK 5   Children write **it**

a. Everybody, get ready to say the sounds in (pause) **it.** Get ready. Signal for each sound as the children say *iiit.*

b. Let's do it the hard way. My turn. Saying the sounds in (pause) **it.** **Iii** (pause two seconds) **t.** I said the sounds the hard way.

c. Do it with me. Saying the sounds in (pause) **it** the hard way. Get ready. Signal for each sound as you and the children say **iii** (pause two seconds) **t.** Repeat until firm.

d. Your turn. All by yourselves. Saying the sounds in (pause) **it** the hard way. Signal for each sound as the children say *iii* (pause) *t.* The children are to pause between the sounds. **Good.**

e. Again. Saying the sounds in (pause) **it** the hard way. Get ready. Signal for each sound as the children say *iii* (pause) *t.* The children are to pause two seconds between the sounds.

f. Everybody, write the sounds in (pause) **it.** Check children's responses. You wrote the word (pause) **it.** What word did you write? (Signal.) *It.*

TASK 6   Children write **at**

a. Everybody, get ready to say the sounds in (pause) **at.** Get ready. Signal for each sound as the children say *aaat.*

b. Let's do it the hard way. My turn. Saying the sounds in (pause) **at.** **Aaa** (pause) **t.** I said the sounds the hard way.

c. Do it with me. Saying the sounds in (pause) **at** the hard way. Get ready. Signal for each sound as you and the children say **aaa** (pause two seconds) **t.** Repeat until firm.

d. Your turn. All by yourselves. Saying the sounds in (pause) **at** the hard way. Get ready. Signal for each sound as the children say *aaa* (pause) *t.* The children are to pause between the sounds. **Good.**

e. Again. Saying the sounds in (pause) **at** the hard way. Get ready. Signal for each sound as the children say *aaa* (pause) *t.* The children are to pause two seconds between the sounds.

f. Everybody, write the sounds in (pause) **at.** Check children's responses. You wrote the word (pause) **at.** What word did you write? (Signal.) *At.*

END OF SPELLING LESSON

Spelling Lesson 11

SOUND WRITING

TASK 1   Children write **n i, r t**

a. Here are the sounds you're going to write. Listen. **nnn** (pause two seconds) **iii.**

b. Listen again. **nnn** (pause two seconds) **iii.**

c. Your turn to say the sounds. Get ready. Clap. *nnn.* (Pause two seconds.) Clap. *iii.* Repeat until firm.

d. What sound are you going to write first? (Signal.) *nnn.*

e. What sound are you going to write next? (Signal.) *iii.*

f. Repeat *d* and *e* until firm.

g. Write **nnn** and **iii.** Check children's responses.

h. Repeat *a* through *g* for **r t.**

TASK 2   Children write **t a n**

a. Here are some sounds you're going to write next. Listen. **t** (pause) **aaa** (pause) **nnn.**

b. Listen again. **t** (pause) **aaa** (pause) **nnn.**

c. Say the sounds with me. Get ready. Clap for each sound as you and the children say **t** (pause) **aaa** (pause) **nnn.** Repeat until firm.

d. What sound are you going to write first? (Signal.) *t.*

e. What sound are you going to write next? (Signal.) *aaa.*

f. What sound are you going to write next? (Signal.) *nnn.*

g. Repeat *d* through *f* until firm.

h. Write **t** (pause) **aaa** (pause) **nnn.** Check children's responses.

SAY THE SOUNDS

TASK 3   Children say the sounds in **in, an**

a. Listen. You're going to say the sounds in the word (pause) **in**.

b. What word? (Signal.) *In.* Yes, **in**.

c. Hold up your hand. **Saying the sounds in** (pause) **in. Get ready.**
Signal for **i** and **n**. The children say *iiinnn* without pausing between the sounds.

d. Again. Repeat *c* until firm.

e. When **iiinnn** is firm, say: **Say it fast.** (Signal.) *In.*

f. Yes, what word? (Signal.) *In.* Good. You said the sounds in
(pause) **in**.

g. Repeat *a* through *f* for **an**.

WORD WRITING

TASK 4   Children write **at**

a. Everybody, get ready to say the sounds in (pause) **at. Get ready.**
Signal for each sound as the children say *aaat*.

b. Let's do it the hard way. My turn. Saying the sounds in (pause) **at.**
Aaa (pause) **t.** I said the sounds the hard way.

c. Do it with me. Saying the sounds in (pause) **at the hard way.**
Get ready. Signal for each sound as you and the children say
aaa (pause two seconds) **t.** Repeat until firm.

d. Your turn. All by yourselves. Saying the sounds in (pause) **at the
hard way. Get ready.** Signal for each sound as the children say
aaa (pause) *t.* The children are to pause between the sounds.
Good.

e. Again. Saying the sounds in (pause) **at the hard way. Get ready.**
Signal for each sound as the children say *aaa* (pause) *t.* The
children are to pause between the sounds.

f. Everybody, write the sounds in (pause) **at.** Check children's
responses. You wrote the word (pause) **at. What word did you
write?** (Signal.) *At.*

TASK 5   Children write **it**

a. Everybody, get ready to say the sounds in (pause) **it. Get ready.**
Signal for each sound as the children say *iiit.*

b. Let's do it the hard way. My turn. Saying the sounds in (pause) **it.**
Iii (pause) **t.** I said the sounds the hard way.

c. Do it with me. Saying the sounds in (pause) **it the hard way.**
Get ready. Signal for each sound as you and the children say
iii (pause two seconds) **t.** Repeat until firm.

d. Your turn. All by yourselves. Saying the sounds in (pause) **it the
hard way. Get ready.** Signal for each sound as the children say
iii (pause) *t.* The children are to pause between the sounds.
Good.

e. Again. Saying the sounds in (pause) **it the hard way. Get ready.**
Signal for each sound as the children say *iii* (pause) *t.* The
children are to pause between the sounds.

f. Everybody, write the sounds in (pause) **it.** Check children's
responses. You wrote the word (pause) **it. What did you write?**
(Signal.) *It.*

END OF SPELLING LESSON

Spelling Lesson 12

SOUND WRITING

TASK 1   Children write **n r, n a**

a. Here are the sounds you're going to write. Listen.
nnn (pause two seconds) **rrr.**

b. Listen again. **nnn** (pause two seconds) **rrr.**

c. Your turn to say the sounds. Get ready. Clap. *nnn.*
(Pause two seconds.) Clap. *rrr.* Repeat until firm.

d. What sound are you going to write first? (Signal.) *nnn.*

e. What sound are you going to write next? (Signal.) *rrr.*

f. Repeat *d* and *e* until firm.

g. Write **nnn** and **rrr.** Check children's responses.

h. Repeat *a* through *g* for **n a**.

TASK 2   Children write t a n

a. Here are some sounds you're going to write next. Listen.

t (pause) **aaa** (pause) **nnn**.

b. Listen again. **t** (pause) **aaa** (pause) **nnn**.
c. Say the sounds with me. Get ready. Clap for each sound as you and the children say **t** (pause) **aaa** (pause) **nnn**. Repeat until firm.
d. What sound are you going to write first? (Signal.) *t*.
e. What sound are you going to write next? (Signal.) *aaa*.
f. What sound are you going to write next? (Signal.) *nnn*.
g. Repeat *d* through *f* until firm.
h. Write **t** (pause) **aaa** (pause) **nnn**. Check children's responses.

WORD WRITING

TASK 3   Children write at

a. You're going to write the word (pause) **at**. First you're going to say the sounds. Then you're going to write the word.
b. Saying the sounds in (pause) **at**. Get ready. Signal for each sound as the children say *aaat*.
c. Now you're going to say the sounds the hard way. Saying the sounds in (pause) **at**. Get ready. Signal for each sound as the children say *aaa* (pause) *t*. The children are to pause two seconds between the sounds.
d. Repeat *c* until firm.
e. Everybody, write the word (pause) **at**. Check children's responses. What word did you write? (Signal.) *At*.

TASK 4   Children write it

a. You're going to write the word (pause) **it**. First you're going to say the sounds. Then you're going to write the word.
b. Saying the sounds in (pause) **it**. Get ready. Signal for each sound as the children say *iiit*.
c. Now you're going to say the sounds the hard way. Saying the sounds in (pause) **it**. Get ready. Signal for each sound as the children say *iii* (pause) *t*. The children are to pause two seconds between the sounds.
d. Repeat *c* until firm.
e. Everybody, write the word (pause) **it**. Check children's responses. What word did you write? (Signal.) *It*.

TASK 5   Children write in

a. You're going to write the word (pause) **in**. First you're going to say the sounds. Then you're going to write the word.
b. Saying the sounds in (pause) **in**. Get ready. Signal for each sound as the children say *iiinnn*.
c. Now you're going to say the sounds the hard way. Saying the sounds in (pause) **in**. Get ready. Signal for each sound as the children say *iii* (pause) *nnn*. The children are to pause two seconds between the sounds.
d. Repeat *c* until firm.
e. Everybody, write the word (pause) **in**. Check children's responses. What word did you write? (Signal.) *In*.

END OF SPELLING LESSON

Spelling Lesson 13

SOUND WRITING

TASK 1   Children write f

a. You're going to write a sound.
b. Here's the sound you're going to write. Listen. **fff**.

What sound? (Signal.) *fff*.

c. Write **fff**. Check children's responses.

TASK 2   Children write r f t, f a i

a. Here are some sounds you're going to write next. Listen.

rrr (pause) **fff** (pause) **t**.

b. Listen again. **rrr** (pause) **fff** (pause) **t**.
c. Say the sounds with me. Get ready. Clap for each sound as you and the children say **rrr** (pause) **fff** (pause) **t**. Repeat until firm.
d. What sound are you going to write first? (Signal.) *rrr*.
e. What sound are you going to write next? (Signal.) *fff*.
f. What sound are you going to write next? (Signal.) *t*.
g. Repeat *d* through *h* until firm.
h. Write **rrr** (pause) **fff** (pause) **t**. Check children's responses.
i. Repeat *a* through *h* for **f a i**.

WORD WRITING

TASK 3   Children write an, in, at

a. **You're going to write the word** (pause) **an. First you're going to say the sounds. Then you're going to write the word.**

b. **Saying the sounds in** (pause) **an. Get ready.** Signal for each sound as the children say *aaannn.*

c. **Now you're going to say the sounds the hard way. Saying the sounds in** (pause) **an. Get ready.** Signal for each sound as the children say *aaa* (pause) *nnn.* The children are to pause two seconds between the sounds.

d. Repeat *c* until firm.

e. **Everybody, write the word** (pause) **an.** Check children's responses. **What word did you write?** (Signal.) *An.*

f. Repeat *a* through *e* for **in** and **at.**

END OF SPELLING LESSON

Spelling Lesson 14

SOUND WRITING

TASK 1   Children write f i n, f a n, f i t

a. **Here are some sounds you're going to write. Listen.** **fff** (pause) **iii** (pause) **nnn.**

b. **Listen again. fff** (pause) **iii** (pause) **nnn.**

c. **Say the sounds with me. Get ready.** Clap for each sound as you and the children say **fff** (pause) **iii** (pause) **nnn** Repeat until firm.

d. **What sound are you going to write first?** (Signal.) *fff.*

e. **What sound are you going to write next?** (Signal.) *iii.*

f. **What sound are you going to write next?** (Signal.) *nnn.*

g. Repeat *d* through *f* until firm.

h. **Write fff** (pause) **iii** (pause) **nnn.** Check children's responses.

i. Repeat *a* through *h* for **f a n.**

j. Repeat *a* through *h* for **f i t.**

WORD WRITING

TASK 2   Children write at, it, rat

a. **You're going to write the word** (pause) **at. First you're going to say the sounds. Then you're going to write the word.**

b. **Saying the sounds in** (pause) **at. Get ready.** Signal for each sound as the children say *aaat.*

c. **Now you're going to say the sounds the hard way. Saying the sounds in** (pause) **at. Get ready.** Signal for each sound as the children say *aaa* (pause) *t.* The children are to pause two seconds between the sounds.

d. Repeat *c* until firm.

e. **Everybody, write the word** (pause) **at.** Check children's responses. **What word did you write?** (Signal.) *At.*

f. Repeat *a* through *e* for **it** and **rat.**

END OF SPELLING LESSON

Spelling Lesson 15

SOUND WRITING

TASK 1   Children write f a n, f a t

a. **Here are some sounds you're going to write. Listen.** **fff** (pause) **aaa** (pause) **nnn.**

b. **Listen again. fff** (pause) **aaa** (pause) **nnn.**

c. **Say the sounds with me. Get ready.** Clap for each sound as you and the children say **fff** (pause) **aaa** (pause) **nnn.** Repeat until firm.

d. **What sound are you going to write first?** (Signal.) *fff.*

e. **What sound are you going to write next?** (Signal.) *aaa.*

f. **What sound are you going to write next?** (Signal.) *nnn.*

g. Repeat *d* through *f* until firm.

h. **Write fff** (pause) **aaa** (pause) **nnn.** Check children's responses.

i. Repeat *a* through *h* for **f a t.**

WORD WRITING

TASK 2   Children write **if, in**

a. You're going to write the word (pause) **if.** First you're going to say the sounds. Then you're going to write the word.

b. Saying the sounds in (pause) **if.** Get ready. Signal for each sound as the children say *iiifff.*

c. Now you're going to say the sounds the hard way. Saying the sounds in (pause) **if.** Get ready. Signal for each sound as the children say *iii* (pause) *fff.* The children are to pause two seconds between the sounds.

d. Repeat *c* until firm.

e. Everybody, write the word (pause) **if.** Check children's responses. **What word did you write?** (Signal.) *If.*

f. Repeat *a* through *e* for **in.**

TASK 3   Children write **it, rat**

a. You're going to write the word **it.** Listen. **It.** Saying the sounds in (pause) **it** the hard way. Get ready. Signal for each sound as the children say *iii* (pause) *t.* The children are to pause two seconds between the sounds. Repeat until firm.

b. Everybody, write the word (pause) **it.** Check children's responses.

c. Now you're going to write the word **rat.** Listen. **Rat.** Saying the sounds the hard way. Get ready. Signal for each sound as the children say *rrr* (pause) *aaa* (pause) *t.* The children are to pause two seconds between the sounds. Repeat until firm.

d. Everybody, write the word (pause) **rat.** Check children's responses.

END OF SPELLING LESSON

Spelling Lesson 16

SOUND WRITING

TASK 1   Children write **o**

a. You're going to write a sound.

b. Here's the sound you're going to write. Listen. **ooo.** **What sound?** (Signal.) *ooo.*

c. Write **ooo.** Check children's responses.

TASK 2   Children write **t i o, n o f**

a. Here are some sounds you're going to write next. Listen. **t** (pause) **iii** (pause) **ooo.**

b. Listen again. **t** (pause) **iii** (pause) **ooo.**

c. Say the sounds with me. Get ready. Clap for each sound as you and the children say **t** (pause) **iii** (pause) **ooo.** Repeat until firm.

d. What sound are you going to write first? (Signal.) *t.*

e. What sound are you going to write next? (Signal.) *iii.*

f. What sound are you going to write next? (Signal.) *ooo.*

g. Repeat *d* through *f* until firm.

h. Write **t** (pause) **iii** (pause) **ooo.** Check children's responses.

i. Repeat *a* through *h* for **n o f.**

WORD WRITING

TASK 3   Children write **an, fan, it**

a. You're going to write the word **an.** Saying the sounds the hard way. Get ready. Signal for each sound as the children say *aaa* (pause) *nnn.* The children are to pause two seconds between the sounds. Repeat until firm.

b. Everybody, write the word (pause) **an.** Check children's responses.

c. Repeat *a* and *b* for **fan** and **it.**

END OF SPELLING LESSON

Spelling Lesson 17

SOUND WRITING

TASK 1   Children write o t i, r o t

a. Here are some sounds you're going to write. Listen.
                                         ooo (pause) **t** (pause) **iii**.
b. Listen again. **ooo** (pause) **t** (pause) **iii**.
c. Say the sounds with me. Get ready. Clap for each sound as you
      and the children say **ooo** (pause) **t** (pause) **iii**. Repeat until
                                                                    firm.
d. What sound are you going to write first? (Signal.) *ooo*.
e. What sound are you going to write next? (Signal.) *t*.
f. What sound are you going to write next? (Signal.) *iii*.
g. Repeat *d* through *f* until firm.
h. Write **ooo** (pause) **t** (pause) **iii**. Check children's responses.
i. Repeat *a* through *h* for **r o t**.

WORD WRITING

TASK 2   Children write an, fan, at, fat

a. You're going to write the word **an**. Listen. **An**. Saying the sounds
      the hard way. Get ready. Signal for each sound as the children
          say *aaa* (pause) *nnn*. The children are to pause two seconds
                                    between the sounds. Repeat until firm.
b. Everybody, write the word (pause) **an**. Check children's responses.
c. Repeat *a* and *b* for **fan, at,** and **fat.**

END OF SPELLING LESSON

Spelling Lesson 18

SOUND WRITING

TASK 1   Children write n o t, n a f

a. Here are some sounds you're going to write. Listen.
                                         nnn (pause) **ooo** (pause) **t**.
b. Listen again. **nnn** (pause) **ooo** (pause) **t**.
c. Say the sounds with me. Get ready. Clap for each sound as you
      and the children say **nnn** (pause) **ooo** (pause) **t**. Repeat until
                                                                    firm.
d. What sound are you going to write first? (Signal.) *nnn*.
e. What sound are you going to write next? (Signal.) *ooo*.
f. What sound are you going to write next? (Signal.) *t*.
g. Repeat *d* through *f* until firm.
h. Write **nnn** (pause) **ooo** (pause) **t**. Check children's responses.
i. Repeat *a* through *h* for **n a f**.

WORD WRITING

TASK 2   Children write in, fin, an, fan

a. You're going to write the word **in**. Listen. **In**. Saying the sounds the
      hard way. Get ready. Signal for each sound as the children say
          iii (pause) *nnn*. The children are to pause two seconds between
                                          the sounds. Repeat until firm.
b. Everybody, write the word (pause) **in**. Check children's responses.
c. Repeat *a* and *b* for **fin, an,** and **fan.**

END OF SPELLING LESSON

Spelling Lesson 19

SOUND WRITING

TASK 1   Children write a n a, t o n

a. Here are some sounds you're going to write. Listen.

                                  aaa   (pause) **nnn**   (pause) **aaa.**

b. Listen again. **aaa**   (pause) **nnn**   (pause) **aaa.**

c. Say the sounds with me. Get ready.   Clap for each sound as you and
     the children say **aaa**   (pause) **nnn**   (pause) **aaa.** Repeat until
                                                                            firm.

d. What sound are you going to write first?   (Signal.) *aaa.*
e. What sound are you going to write next?   (Signal.) *nnn.*
f. What sound are you going to write next?   (Signal.) *aaa.*
g. Repeat *d* through *f* until firm.
h. Write **aaa**   (pause) **nnn**   (pause) **aaa.**   Check children's responses.
i. Repeat *a* through *h* for **t o n.**

WORD WRITING

TASK 2   Children write rat, if, it, in

a. You're going to write the word **rat**. Listen. **Rat.** Saying the sounds
     the hard way. Get ready.   Signal for each sound as the children
         say *rrr* (pause) *aaa* (pause) *t.* The children are to pause two
                   seconds between the sounds. Repeat until firm.
b. Everybody, write the word   (pause) **rat.**   Check children's
                                                                        responses.

c. Repeat *a* and *b* for **if, it,** and **in.**

END OF SPELLING LESSON

Spelling Lesson 20

SOUND WRITING

TASK 1   Children write m

a. You're going to write a sound.
b. Here's the sound you're going to write. Listen. **mmm.**
                                  What sound?   (Signal.) *mmm.*
c. Write **mmm.**   Check children's responses.

TASK 2   Children write a n m, o m i

a. Here are some sounds you're going to write next. Listen.

                                  aaa   (pause) **nnn**   (pause) **mmm.**

b. Listen again. **aaa**   (pause) **nnn**   (pause) **mmm.**

c. Say the sounds with me. Get ready.   Clap for each sound as you and
     the children say **aaa**   (pause) **nnn**   (pause) **mmm.** Repeat
                                                                   until firm.

d. What sound are you going to write first?   (Signal.) *aaa.*
e. What sound are you going to write next?   (Signal.) *nnn.*
f. What sound are you going to write next?   (Signal.) *mmm.*
g. Repeat *d* through *f* until firm.
h. Write **aaa**   (pause) **nnn**   (pause) **mmm.**   Check children's
                                                                    responses.

i. Repeat *a* through *h* for **o m i.**

SOUND WRITING

TASK 3   Children write an, fan, ran, if

a. You're going to write the word **an**. Listen. **An.** Saying the sounds
     the hard way. Get ready.   Signal for each sound as the children
         say *aaa* (pause) *nnn.* The children are to pause two seconds
                             between the sounds. Repeat until firm.
b. Everybody, write the word   (pause) **an.**   Check children's responses.
c. Repeat *a* and *b* for **fan, ran,** and **if.**

END OF SPELLING LESSON

Spelling Lesson 21

SOUND WRITING

TASK 1   Children write **o m i, f m t**

a. Here are some sounds you're going to write. Listen.
ooo (pause) **mmm** (pause) **iii.**

b. Listen again. **ooo** (pause) **mmm** (pause) **iii.**

c. Say the sounds with me. Get ready. Clap for each sound as you
and the children say **ooo** (pause) **mmm** (pause) **iii.** Repeat
until firm.

d. What sound are you going to write first? (Signal.) *ooo.*

e. What sound are you going to write next? (Signal.) *mmm.*

f. What sound are you going to write next? (Signal.) *iii.*

g. Repeat *d* through *f* until firm.

h. Write **ooo** (pause) **mmm** (pause) **iii.** Check children's responses.

i. Repeat *a* through *h* for **f m t.**

WORD WRITING

TASK 2   Children write **it**

You're going to write the word **it**. Think about the sounds in (pause)
it and write the word. Check children's responses.

To correct	1. Say the sounds in **it**. (Signal.) *liit.*
	2. Say the sounds the hard way. (Signal.) *lii* (pause) *t.*
	3. Write the word **it**. Check children's responses.

TASK 3   Children write **fit**

a. Now you're going to write the word **fit**. Listen. **Fit.** Saying the
sounds the hard way. Get ready. Signal for each sound as the
children say *fff* (pause) *iii* (pause) *t.* The children are to pause
two seconds between the sounds. Repeat until firm.

b. Everybody, write the word (pause) **fit**. Check children's responses.

TASK 4   Children write **at**

You're going to write the word **at**. Think about the sounds in (pause)
at and write the word. Check children's responses.

TASK 5   Children write **fat**

a. Now you're going to write the word **fat**. Listen. **Fat.** Saying the
sounds the hard way. Get ready. Signal for each sound as the
children say *fff* (pause) *aaa* (pause) *t.* The children are to pause
two seconds between the sounds. Repeat until firm.

b. Everybody, write the word (pause) **fat**. Check children's responses.

END OF SPELLING LESSON

Spelling Lesson 22

SOUND WRITING

TASK 1   Children write **o n m, a t m**

a. Here are some sounds you're going to write. Listen.
ooo (pause) **nnn** (pause) **mmm.**

b. Listen again. **ooo** (pause) **nnn** (pause) **mmm.**

c. Say the sounds with me. Get ready. Clap for each sound as you
and the children say **ooo** (pause) **nnn** (pause) **mmm.** Repeat
until firm.

d. What sound are you going to write first? (Signal.) *ooo.*

e. What sound are you going to write next? (Signal.) *nnn.*

f. What sound are you going to write next? (Signal.) *mmm.*

g. Repeat *d* through *f* until firm.

h. Write **ooo** (pause) **nnn** (pause) **mmm.** Check children's
responses.

i. Repeat *a* through *h* for **a t m.**

WORD WRITING

TASK 2 Children write **in**

You're going to write the word **in**. Think about the sounds in (pause) **in** and write the word. Check children's responses.

To correct	1. Say the sounds in **in**. (Signal.) *Iiinnn*.
	2. Say the sounds the hard way. (Signal.) *Iii* (pause) *nnn*.
	3. Write the word **in**. Check children's responses.

TASK 3 Children write **fin**

a. Now you're going to write the word **fin**. Listen. **Fin**. Saying the sounds the hard way. Get ready. Signal for each sound as the children say *fff* (pause) *iii* (pause) *nnn*. The children are to pause two seconds between the sounds. Repeat until firm.

b. Everybody, write the word (pause) **fin**. Check children's responses.

TASK 4 Children write **an**

You're going to write the word **an**. Think about the sounds in (pause) **an** and write the word. Check children's responses.

TASK 5 Children write **ran**

a. Now you're going to write the word **ran**. Listen. **Ran**. Saying the sounds the hard way. Get ready. Signal for each sound as the children say *rrr* (pause) *aaa* (pause) *nnn*. The children are to pause two seconds between the sounds. Repeat until firm.

b. Everybody, write the word (pause) **ran**. Check children's responses.

END OF SPELLING LESSON

Spelling Lesson 23

SOUND WRITING

TASK 1 Children write **m n o, n m r**

a. Here are some sounds you're going to write. Listen. **mmm** (pause) **nnn** (pause) **ooo**.

b. Listen again. **mmm** (pause) **nnn** (pause) **ooo**.

c. Say the sounds with me. Get ready. Clap for each sound as you and the children say **mmm** (pause) **nnn** (pause) **ooo**. Repeat until firm.

d. What sound are you going to write first? (Signal.) *mmm*.

e. What sound are you going to write next? (Signal.) *nnn*.

f. What sound are you going to write next? (Signal.) *ooo*.

g. Repeat *d* through *f* until firm.

h. Write **mmm** (pause) **nnn** (pause) **ooo**. Check responses.

i. Repeat *a* through *h* for **n m r**.

WORD WRITING

TASK 2 Children write **an**

You're going to write the word **an**. Think about the sounds in (pause) **an** and write the word. Check children's responses.

To correct	1. Say the sounds in **an**. (Signal.) *Aaannn*.
	2. Say the sounds the hard way. (Signal.) *Aaa* (pause) *nnn*.
	3. Write the word **an**. Check children's responses.

TASK 3 Children write **fan, ran, man**

a. Now you're going to write the word **fan**. Listen. **Fan**. Saying the sounds the hard way. Get ready. Signal for each sound as the children say *fff* (pause) *aaa* (pause) *nnn*. The children are to pause two seconds between sounds. Repeat until firm.

b. Everybody, write the word (pause) **fan**. Check responses.

c. Repeat *a* and *b* for **ran** and **man**.

END OF SPELLING LESSON

Spelling Lesson 24

SOUND WRITING

TASK 1   Children write o t m, f r i

a. Here are some sounds you're going to write. Listen.
ooo (pause) t (pause) mmm.
b. Listen again. ooo. (pause) t (pause) mmm.
c. Say the sounds with me. Get ready. Clap for each sound as you and the children say ooo (pause) t (pause) mmm. Repeat until firm.
d. What sound are you going to write first? (Signal.) *ooo.*
e. What sound are you going to write next? (Signal.) *t.*
f. What sound are you going to write next? (Signal.) *mmm.*
g. Repeat *d* through *f* until firm.
h. Write ooo (pause) t (pause) mmm. Check children's responses.
i. Repeat *a* through *h* for f r i.

WORD WRITING

TASK 2   Children write at

You're going to write the word at. Think about the sounds in (pause) at and write the word. Check children's responses.

To correct	1. Say the sounds in at. (Signal.) *Aaat.*
	2. Say the sounds the hard way. (Signal.) *Aaa* (pause) *t.*
	3. Write the word at. Check children's responses.

TASK 3   Children write mat

a. You're going to write the word mat. Listen. Mat. Saying the sounds in (pause) mat the hard way. Get ready. Signal for each sound as the children say *mmm* (pause) *aaa* (pause) *t.* The children are to pause two seconds between the sounds. Repeat until firm.
b. Everybody, write the word (pause) mat. Check children's responses.

TASK 4   Children write am

You're going to write the word am. Think about the sounds in (pause) am and write the word. Check children's responses.

TASK 5   Children write ram

a. You're going to write the word ram. Listen. Ram. Saying the sounds in (pause) ram the hard way. Get ready. Signal for each sound as the children say *rrr* (pause) *aaa* (pause) *mmm.* The children are to pause two seconds between the sounds. Repeat until firm.
b. Everybody, write the word (pause) ram. Check children's responses.

TASK 6   Children write in

You're going to write the word in. Think about the sounds in (pause) in and write the word. Check children's responses.

END OF SPELLING LESSON

Spelling Lesson 25

SOUND WRITING

TASK 1   Children write a m i

a. Here are some sounds you're going to write. Listen.
aaa (pause) mmm (pause) iii.
b. Listen again. aaa (pause) mmm (pause) iii.
c. Say the sounds with me. Get ready. Clap for each sound as you and the children say aaa (pause) mmm (pause) iii. Repeat until firm.
d. What sound are you going to write first? (Signal.) *aaa.*
e. What sound are you going to write next? (Signal.) *mmm.*
f. What sound are you going to write next? (Signal.) *iii.*
g. Repeat *d* through *f* until firm.
h. Write aaa (pause) mmm (pause) iii. Check children's responses.

WORD WRITING

TASK 2 Children write **if**, **it**

a. You're going to write the word **if**. Think about the sounds in (pause) **if** and write the word. Check children's responses.

To correct	1. Say the sounds in **if**. (Signal.) *liifff*.
	2. Say the sounds the hard way. (Signal.) *lii* (pause) *fff*.
	3. Write the word **if**. Check children's responses.

b. Repeat *a* for **it**.

TASK 3 Children write **on**

a. You're going to write the word **on**. Listen. **On**. Saying the sounds in (pause) **on** the hard way. Get ready. Signal for each sound as the children say *ooo* (pause) *nnn*. The children are to pause two seconds between the sounds. Repeat until firm.

b. Everybody, write the word (pause) **on**. Check children's responses.

TASK 4 Children write **at**

You're going to write the word **at**. Think about the sounds in (pause) **at** and write the word. Check children's responses.

TASK 5 Children write **mat**, **ram**

a. You're going to write the word **mat**. Listen. **Mat**. Saying the sounds in (pause) **mat** the hard way. Get ready. Signal for each sound as the children say *mmm* (pause) *aaa* (pause) *t*. The children are to pause two seconds between the sounds. Repeat until firm.

b. Everybody, write the word (pause) **mat**. Check children's responses.

c. Repeat *a* and *b* for **ram**.

END OF SPELLING LESSON

Spelling Lesson 26

WORD WRITING

TASK 1 Children write **an**

You're going to write the word **an**. Think about the sounds in (pause) **an** and write the word. Check children's responses.

To correct	1. Say the sounds in **an**. (Signal.) *Aaannn*.
	2. Say the sounds the hard way. (Signal.) *Aaa* (pause) *nnn*.
	3. Write the word **an**. Check children's responses.

TASK 2 Children write **fan**, **ran**

a. You're going to write the word **fan**. Listen. **Fan**. Saying the sounds in (pause) **fan** the hard way. Get ready. Signal for each sound as the children say *fff* (pause) *aaa* (pause) *nnn*. The children are to pause two seconds between the sounds. Repeat until firm.

b. Everybody, write the word (pause) **fan**. Check children's responses.

c. Repeat *a* and *b* for **ran**.

TASK 3 Children write **man**, **it**

a. You're going to write the word **man**. Think about the sounds in (pause) **man** and write the word. Check children's responses.

b. Repeat *a* for **it**.

TASK 4 Children write **fit**, **on**

a. You're going to write the word **fit**. Listen. **Fit**. Saying the sounds in (pause) **fit** the hard way. Get ready. Signal for each sound as the children say *fff* (pause) *iii* (pause) *t*. The children are to pause two seconds between the sounds. Repeat until firm.

b. Everybody, write the word (pause) **fit**. Check children's responses.

c. Repeat *a* and *b* for **on**.

END OF SPELLING LESSON

Spelling Lesson 27

WORD WRITING

TASK 1   Children write **am, an, ran, fan, man**

a. You're going to write the word **am**. Think about the sounds in (pause) **am** and write the word. Check children's responses.

To correct	1. Say the sounds in **am**. (Signal.) *Aaammm.* 2. Say the sounds the hard way. (Signal.) *Aaa* (pause) *mmm.* 3. Write the word **am**. Check children's responses.

b. Repeat *a* for the following words: **an, ran, fan, man.**

TASK 2   Children write **fit, ron**

a. You're going to write the word **fit**. Listen. **Fit**. Saying the sounds in (pause) **fit** the hard way. Get ready. Signal for each sound as the children say *fff* (pause) *iii* (pause) *t*. The children are to pause two seconds between the sounds. Repeat until firm.

b. Everybody, write the word (pause) **fit**. Check children's responses.

c. Repeat *a* and *b* for **ron**.

END OF SPELLING LESSON

Spelling Lesson 28

WORD WRITING

TASK 1   Children write **an, man, on, ron**

a. You're going to write the word **an**. Think about the sounds in (pause) **an** and write the word. Check children's responses.

To correct	1. Say the sounds in **an**. (Signal.) *Aaannn.* 2. Say the sounds the hard way. (Signal.) *Aaa* (pause) *nnn.* 3. Write the word **an**. Check children's responses.

b. Repeat *a* for **man, on,** and **ron.**

TASK 2   Children write **mat**

a. You're going to write the word **mat**. Listen. **Mat**. Saying the sounds in (pause) **mat** the hard way. Get ready. Signal for each sound as the children say *mmm* (pause) *aaa* (pause) *t*. The children are to pause two seconds between the sounds. Repeat until firm.

b. Everybody, write the word (pause) **mat**. Check children's responses.

TASK 3   Children write **it, fit**

a. You're going to write the word **it**. Think about the sounds in (pause) **it** and write the word. Check children's responses.

b. Repeat *a* for **fit**.

END OF SPELLING LESSON

Spelling Lesson 29

WORD WRITING

TASK   Children write **am, ram, in, fin, on, ron, it, fit**

a. You're going to write the word **am**. Think about the sounds in (pause) **am** and write the word. Check children's responses.

To correct	1. Say the sounds in **am**. (Signal.) *Aaammm.* 2. Say the sounds the hard way. (Signal.) *Aaa* (pause) *mmm.* 3. Write the word **am**. Check children's responses.

b. Repeat *a* for the following words: **ram, in, fin, on, ron, it, fit.**

END OF SPELLING LESSON

Spelling Lesson 30

WORD WRITING

TASK Children write **in**, **fin**, **at**, **mat**, **an**, **man**, **on**, **ron**

a. You're going to write the word **in**. Think about the sounds in (pause) **in** and write the word. Check children's responses.

To correct	1. Say the sounds in **in**. (Signal.) *Iiinnn.* 2. Say the sounds the hard way. (Signal.) *Iii* (pause) *nnn.* 3. Write the word **in**. Check children's responses.

b. Repeat *a* for the following words: **fin, at, mat, an, man, on, ron.**

END OF SPELLING LESSON

Spelling Lesson 31

SOUND WRITING

TASK 1 Children write **s**

a. You're going to write a sound.
b. Here's the sound you're going to write. Listen. **sss.**
What sound? (Signal.) *sss.*

c. Write **sss.** Check children's responses.

TASK 2 Children write **it**, **if**, **in**, **on**, **an**, **am**, **at**

a. You're going to write the word **it**. Think about the sounds in (pause) **it** and write the word. Check children's responses.

To correct	1. Say the sounds in **it**. (Signal.) *Iiit.* 2. Say the sounds the hard way. (Signal.) *Iii* (pause) *t.* 3. Write the word **it**. Check children's responses.

b. Repeat *a* for the following words: **if, in, on, an, am, at.**

END OF SPELLING LESSON

Spelling Lesson 32

SOUND WRITING

TASK 1 Children write **s**

a. You're going to write a sound.
b. Here's the sound you're going to write. Listen. **sss.**
What sound? (Signal.) *sss.*

c. Write **sss.** Check children's responses.

TASK 2 Children write **if**, **it**, **sit**, **at**, **sat**, **in**, **sin**

a. You're going to write the word **if**. Think about the sounds in (pause) **if** and write the word. Check children's responses.

To correct	1. Say the sounds in **if**. (Signal.) *Iiifff.* 2. Say the sounds the hard way. (Signal.) *Iii* (pause) *fff.* 3. Write the word **if**. Check children's responses.

b. Repeat *a* for the following words: **it, sit, at, sat, in, sin.**

END OF SPELLING LESSON

Spelling Lesson 33

WORD WRITING

TASK 1 Children write **an**, **am**, **mat**, **if**, **it**, **in**, **sin**

a. You're going to write the word **an**. Think about the sounds in (pause) **an** and write the word. Check children's responses.

To correct	1. Say the sounds in **an**. (Signal.) *Aaannn.* 2. Say the sounds the hard way. (Signal.) *Aaa* (pause) *nnn.* 3. Write the word **an**. Check children's responses.

b. Repeat *a* for the following words: **am, mat, if, it, in, sin.**

TASK 2 Children write is

a. You're going to write the word   (pause) **is.** When you write the word   (pause) **is,** you write these sounds. **Iii**   (pause) **sss.**

b. Say the sounds you write for   (pause) **is.** Get ready.

 Signal for each sound as the children say *iii* (pause) *sss.* The children are to pause two seconds between the sounds. Repeat until firm.

c. Everybody, write the word   (pause) **is.** Check children's responses.

END OF SPELLING LESSON

Spelling Lesson 34

SOUND WRITING

TASK 1   Children write **h**

a. You're going to write a sound.

b. Here's the sound you're going to write. Listen. **h.**

     What sound? (Signal.) *h.*

c. Write **h.** Check children's responses.

WORD WRITING

TASK 2   Children write **am, ram**

a. You're going to write the word **am.** Think about the sounds in (pause) **am** and write the word. Check children's responses.

To correct	1. Say the sounds in **am**. (Signal.) *Aaammm.*
	2. Say the sounds the hard way. (Signal.) *Aaa* (pause) *mmm.*
	3. Write the word **am**. Check children's responses.

b. Repeat *a* for **ram.**

TASK 3 Children write is

a. You're going to write the word   (pause) **is.** When you write the word   (pause) **is,** you write these sounds. **Iii**   (pause) **sss.**

b. Say the sounds you write for   (pause) **is.** Get ready.

 Signal for each sound as the children say *iii* (pause) *sss.* The children are to pause two seconds between the sounds. Repeat until firm.

c. Everybody, write the word   (pause) **is.** Check children's responses.

TASK 4   Children write **if, an, on, it, at**

a. You're going to write the word **if.** Think about the sounds in (pause) **if** and write the word. Check children's responses.

To correct	1. Say the sounds in **if**. (Signal.) *Iiifff.*
	2. Say the sounds the hard way. (Signal.) *Iii* (pause) *fff.*
	3. Write the word **if**. Check children's responses.

b. Repeat *a* for the following words: **an, on, it, at.**

END OF SPELLING LESSON

Spelling Lesson 35

SOUND WRITING

TASK 1   Children write **h**

a. You're going to write a sound.

b. Here's the sound you're going to write. Listen. **h.**

     What sound? (Signal.) *h.*

c. Write **h.** Check children's responses.

WORD WRITING

TASK 2 Children write **is**

a. You're going to write the word   (pause) **is**. When you write the
word   (pause) **is**, you write these sounds. **Iii** (pause) **sss**.
b. Say the sounds you write for   (pause) **is**. Get ready.
Signal for each sound as the children say *iii* (pause) *sss*. The
children are to pause two seconds between the sounds. Repeat
until firm.

c. Everybody, write the word   (pause) **is**.   Check children's responses.

TASK 3 Children write **at, sat, it, sit, in, sin**

a. You're going to write the word **at**. Think about the sounds in
(pause) **at** and write the word.   Check children's responses.

To correct	1. Say the sounds in **at**. (Signal.) *Aaat.*
	2. Say the sounds the hard way. (Signal.) *Aaa* (pause) *t.*
	3. Write the word **at**. Check children's responses.

b. Repeat *a* for the following words: **sat, it, sit, in**, and **sin**.

END OF SPELLING LESSON

Spelling Lesson 36

WORD WRITING

TASK 1 Children write **it, sit**

a. You're going to write the word **it**. Think about the sounds in
(pause) **it** and write the word.   Check children's responses.

To correct	1. Say the sounds in **it**. (Signal.) *Iiit.*
	2. Say the sounds the hard way. (Signal.) *Iii* (pause) *t.*
	3. Write the word **it**. Check children's responses.

b. Repeat *a* for **sit**.

TASK 2 Children write **hit**

a. You're going to write the word   (pause) **hit**. This word is tough.
I'll say the sounds in   (pause) **hit** the hard way. Listen.
H   (pause one second) *iii*   (pause one second) *t.*
b. Your turn. Say the sounds in   (pause) **hit**. Get ready.
Signal for each sound as the children say *h* (pause) *iii* (pause) *t.*
The children are to pause two seconds between the sounds.
Repeat until firm.

c. Everybody, write the word   (pause) **hit**.   Check children's responses.

TASK 3 Children write **at, fat, rat**

a. You're going to write the word **at**. Think about the sounds in
(pause) **at** and write the word.   Check children's responses.
b. Repeat *a* for **fat** and **rat**.

TASK 4 Children write **hat**

a. You're going to write the word   (pause) **hat**. This word is tough.
I'll say the sounds in   (pause) **hat** the hard way. Listen.
H   (pause one second) *aaa*   (pause one second) *t.*
b. Your turn. Say the sounds in   (pause) **hat**. Get ready.
Signal for each sound as the children say *h* (pause) *aaa* (pause) *t.*
The children are to pause two seconds between sounds. Repeat
until firm.

c. Everybody, write the word   (pause) **hat**.   Check children's
responses.

TASK 5 Children write **is**

a. You're going to write the word   (pause) **is**. When you write the
word   (pause) **is**, you write these sounds. **Iii**   (pause) **sss**.
b. Say the sounds you write for   (pause) **is**. Get ready.
Signal for each sound as the children say *iii* (pause) *sss*. The
children are to pause two seconds between the sounds. Repeat
until firm.

c. Everybody, write the word   (pause) **is**.   Check children's responses.

END OF SPELLING LESSON

Spelling Lesson 37

WORD WRITING

TASK 1 Children write **am**, **sam**

a. You're going to write the word **am**. Think about the sounds in (pause) **am** and write the word. Check children's responses.

To correct	1. Say the sounds in **am**. (Signal.) *Aaammm.*
	2. Say the sounds the hard way. (Signal.) *Aaa* (pause) *mmm.*
	3. Write the word **am**. Check children's responses.

b. Repeat *a* for **sam**.

TASK 2 Children write **ham**

a. You're going to write the word (pause) **ham**. This word is tough. I'll say the sounds in (pause) **ham** the hard way. Listen. **H** (pause one second) **aaa** (pause one second) **mmm**.

b. Your turn. Say the sounds in (pause) **ham**. Get ready.
Signal for each sound as the children say *h* (pause) *aaa* (pause) *mmm*. The children are to pause two seconds between the sounds. Repeat until firm.

c. Everybody, write the word (pause) **ham**. Check responses.

TASK 3 Children write **it**

You're going to write the word **it**. Think about the sounds in (pause) **it** and write the word. Check children's responses.

TASK 4 Children write **hit**

a. You're going to write the word (pause) **hit**. This word is tough. I'll say the sounds in (pause) **hit** the hard way. Listen. **H** (pause one second) **iii** (pause one second) **t**.

b. Your turn. Say the sounds in (pause) **hit**. Get ready.
Signal for each sound as the children say *h* (pause) *iii* (pause) *t*. The children are to pause two seconds between the sounds. Repeat until firm.

c. Everybody, write the word (pause) **hit**. Check children's responses.

TASK 5 Children write **an**, **fan**

a. You're going to write the word **an**. Think about the sounds in (pause) **an** and write the word. Check children's responses.

b. Repeat *a* for **fan**.

TASK 6 Children write **is**

a. You're going to write the word (pause) **is**. Say the sounds you write for (pause) **is**. Get ready. Signal for each sound as the children say *iii* (pause) *sss*. The children are to pause two seconds between the sounds. Repeat until firm.

b. Everybody, write the word (pause) **is**. Check children's responses.

END OF SPELLING LESSON

Spelling Lesson 38

WORD WRITING

TASK 1 Children write **am**

You're going to write the word **am**. Think about the sounds in (pause) **am** and write the word. Check children's responses.

To correct	1. Say the sounds in **am**. (Signal.) *Aaammm.*
	2. Say the sounds the hard way. (Signal.) *Aaa* (pause) *mmm.*
	3. Write the word **am**. Check children's responses.

TASK 2 Children write **ham**

a. You're going to write the word (pause) **ham**. This word is tough. I'll say the sounds in (pause) **ham** the hard way. Listen. **H** (pause one second) **aaa** (pause one second) **mmm**.

b. Your turn. Say the sounds in (pause) **ham**. Get ready.
Signal for each sound as the children say *h* (pause) *aaa* (pause) *mmm*. The children are to pause two seconds between the sounds. Repeat until firm.

c. Everybody, write the word (pause) **ham**. Check responses.

TASK 3   Children write it

You're going to write the word **it**. Think about the sounds in (pause) **it** and write the word. Check children's responses.

TASK 4   Children write hit

a. Now you're going to write the word (pause) **hit**. This word is tough. I'll say the sounds in (pause) **hit** the hard way. Listen. **H** (pause one second) **iii** (pause one second) **t.**

b. Your turn. Say the sounds in (pause) **hit**. Get ready. Signal for each sound as the children say *h* (pause) *iii* (pause) *t*. The children are to pause two seconds between the sounds. Repeat until firm.

c. Everybody, write the word (pause) **hit**. Check children's responses.

TASK 5   Children write is

a. Everybody, you're going to write the word (pause) **is**. Say the sounds you write for (pause) **is**. Get ready. Signal for each sound as the children say *iii* (pause) *sss*. The children are to pause two seconds between the sounds. Repeat until firm.

b. Everybody, write the word (pause) **is**. Check children's responses.

TASK 6   Children write his, has

a. You're going to write the word (pause) **his**. When you write the word (pause) **his**, you write these sounds: **H** (pause) **iii** (pause) **sss.**

b. Say the sounds you write for (pause) **his**. Get ready. Signal for each sound as the children say *h* (pause) *iii* (pause) *sss*. The children are to pause two seconds between the sounds. Repeat until firm.

c. Everybody, write the word (pause) **his**. Check responses.

d. You're going to write the word (pause) **has**. When you write the word (pause) **has**, you write these sounds: **H** (pause) **aaa** (pause) **sss.**

e. Say the sounds you write for (pause) **has**. Signal for each sound as the children say *h* (pause) *aaa* (pause) *sss*. The children are to pause two seconds between the sounds. Repeat until firm.

f. Everybody, write the word (pause) **has**. Check responses.

TASK 7   Children write on

You're going to write the word **on**. Think about the sounds in (pause) **on** and write the word. Check children's responses.

END OF SPELLING LESSON

Spelling Lesson 39

WORD WRITING

TASK 1   Children write at

You're going to write the word **at**. Think about the sounds in (pause) **at** and write the word. Check children's responses.

To correct	1. Say the sounds in **at**. (Signal.) *Aaat*.
	2. Say the sounds the hard way. (Signal.) *Aaa* (pause) *t*.
	3. Write the word **at**. Check children's responses.

TASK 2   Children write hat

a. You're going to write the word (pause) **hat**. This word is tough. I'll say the sounds in (pause) **hat** the hard way. Listen. **H** (pause) **aaa** (pause) **t.**

b. Your turn. Say the sounds in (pause) **hat**. Get ready. Signal for each sound as the children say *h* (pause) *aaa* (pause) *t*. The children are to pause two seconds between the sounds. Repeat until firm.

c. Everybody, write the word (pause) **hat**. Check children's responses.

TASK 3   Children write it

You're going to write the word **it**. Think about the sounds in (pause) **it** and write the word. Check children's responses.

TASK 4 Children write **hit**

a. You're going to write the word (pause) **hit**. This word is tough.
I'll say the sounds in (pause) **hit** the hard way. Listen.
H (pause) *iii* (pause) **t**.

b. Your turn. Say the sounds in (pause) **hit**. Get ready.
Signal for each sound as the children say *h* (pause) *iii* (pause) *t*.
The children are to pause two seconds between the sounds.
Repeat until firm.

c. Everybody, write the word (pause) **hit**. Check children's
responses.

TASK 5 Children write **is, his**

a. You're going to write the word (pause) **is**. Say the sounds you
write for (pause) **is**. Get ready. Signal for each sound as the
children say *iii* (pause) *sss*. The children are to pause two
seconds between the sounds. Repeat until firm.

b. Everybody, write the word (pause) **is**. Check children's responses.

c. Now, you're going to write the word (pause) **his**. Say the sounds
you write for (pause) **his**. Get ready. Signal for each sound as
the children say *h* (pause) *iii* (pause) *sss*. The children are to
pause two seconds between the sounds. Repeat until firm.

d. Everybody, write the word (pause) **his**. Check children's
responses.

TASK 6 Children write **has**

a. You're going to write the word (pause) **has**. When you write the
word (pause) **has**, you write these sounds. **H** (pause) **aaa**
(pause) **sss**.

b. Say the sounds you write for (pause) **has**. Get ready. Signal for
each sound as the children say *h* (pause) *aaa* (pause) *sss*. The
children are to pause two seconds between the sounds. Repeat
until firm.

c. Everybody, write the word (pause) **has**. Check children's
responses.

TASK 7 Children write **ham**

a. You're going to write the word (pause) **ham**. This word is tough.
I'll say the sounds in (pause) **ham** the hard way. Listen.
H (pause) **aaa** (pause) **mmm**.

b. Your turn. Say the sounds in (pause) **ham**. Get ready.
Signal for each sound as the children say *h* (pause) *aaa* (pause)
mmm. The children are to pause two seconds between the sounds.
Repeat until firm.

c. Everybody, write the word (pause) **ham**. Check children's
responses.

END OF SPELLING LESSON

Spelling Lesson 40

WORD WRITING

TASK 1 Children write **not, rot**

a. You're going to write the word **not**. Listen. **Not**. Saying the sounds
in (pause) **not** the hard way. Get ready. Signal for each sound
as the children say *nnn* (pause) *ooo* (pause) *t*. The children are to
pause two seconds between the sounds. Repeat until firm.

b. Everybody, write the word (pause) **not**. Check children's
responses.

c. Repeat *a* and *b* for **rot**.

TASK 2 Children write **hot**

a. You're going to write the word (pause) **hot**. This word is tough.
I'll say the sounds in (pause) **hot** the hard way. Listen.
H (pause) **ooo** (pause) **t**.

b. Your turn. Say the sounds in (pause) **hot**. Get ready.
Signal for each sound as the children say *h* (pause) *ooo* (pause) *t*.
The children are to pause two seconds between the sounds.
Repeat until firm.

c. Everybody, write the word (pause) **hot**. Check children's
responses.

TASK 3 Children write rat, fat

a. You're going to write the word **rat**. Think about the sounds in (pause) **rat** and write the word. Check children's responses.

To correct	1. Say the sounds in **rat**. (Signal.) *Rrraaat.*
	2. Say the sounds the hard way. (Signal.) *Rrr* (pause) *aaa* (pause) *t.*
	3. Write the word **rat**. Check children's responses.

b. Repeat *a* for **fat**.

TASK 4 Children write hat

a. You're going to write the word (pause) **hat**. This word is tough. I'll say the sounds in (pause) **hat** the hard way. Listen. **H** (pause) **aaa** (pause) **t.**

b. Your turn. Say the sounds in (pause) **hat**. Get ready. Signal for each sound as the children say *h* (pause) *aaa* (pause) *t.* The children are to pause two seconds between the sounds. Repeat until firm.

c. Everybody, write the word (pause) **hat**. Check children's responses.

TASK 5 Children write is, his

a. You're going to write the word (pause) **is**. Say the sounds you write for (pause) **is**. Get ready. Signal for each sound as the children say *iii* (pause) *sss.* The children are to pause two seconds between the sounds. Repeat until firm.

b. Everybody, write the word (pause) **is**. Check children's responses.

c. Now, you're going to write the word (pause) **his**. Say the sounds you write for (pause) **his**. Get ready. Signal for each sound as the children say *h* (pause) *iii* (pause) *sss.* The children are to pause two seconds between the sounds. Repeat until firm.

d. Everybody, write the word (pause) **his**. Check children's responses.

END OF SPELLING LESSON

Spelling Lesson 41

WORD WRITING

TASK 1 Children write hat, hot

a. You're going to write the word (pause) **hat**. This word is tough. I'll say the sounds in (pause) **hat** the hard way. Listen. **H** (pause) **aaa** (pause) **t.**

b. Your turn. Say the sounds in (pause) **hat**. Get ready. Signal for each sound as the children say *h* (pause) *aaa* (pause) *t.* The children are to pause two seconds between the sounds. Repeat until firm.

c. Everybody, write the word (pause) **hat**. Check children's responses.

d. Now, you're going to write the word (pause) **hot**. This word is tough. I'll say the sounds in (pause) **hot** the hard way. Listen. **H** (pause) **ooo** (pause) **t.**

e. Your turn. Say the sounds in (pause) **hot**. Get ready. Signal for each sound as the children say *h* (pause) *ooo* (pause) *t.* The children are to pause two seconds between the sounds. Repeat until firm.

f. Everybody, write the word (pause) **hot**. Check responses.

TASK 2 Children write hit, ham

a. You're going to write the word **hit**. Think about the sounds in (pause) **hit** and write the word. Check children's responses.

To correct	1. Say the sounds in **hit**. (Signal.) *Hiiit.*
	2. Say the sounds the hard way. (Signal.) *H* (pause) *iii* (pause) *t.*
	3. Write the word **hit**. Check children's responses.

b. Repeat *a* for **ham**.

TASK 3 Children write has

a. You're going to write the word (pause) **has**. Say the sounds you write for (pause) **has**. Get ready. Signal for each sound as the children say *h* (pause) *aaa* (pause) *sss.* The children are to pause two seconds between the sounds. Repeat until firm.

b. Everybody, write the word (pause) **has**. Check responses.

TASK 4   Children write sat, sit, not

a. You're going to write the word **sat**. Think about the sounds in
    (pause) **sat** and write the word.   Check children's responses.
b. Repeat *a* for **sit** and **not**.

END OF SPELLING LESSON

Spelling Lesson 42

WORD WRITING

TASK 1   Children write at, is, on, not, if

a. You're going to write the word **at**. Think about the sounds in
    (pause) **at** and write the word.   Check children's responses.

To correct	1. Say the sounds in **at**. (Signal.) *Aaat*. 2. Say the sounds the hard way. (Signal.) *Aaa* (pause) *t*. 3. Write the word **at**. Check children's responses.

b. You're going to write the word **is**. Think about the sounds in
    (pause) **is** and write the word.   Check children's responses.

To correct	1. Say the sounds the hard way. (Signal.) *Iii* (pause) *sss*. 2. Write the word **is**. Check children's responses.

c. Repeat *a* for **on**, **not**, and **if**.

TASK 2   Children write hot

a. You're going to write the word (pause) **hot**. This word is tough.
    I'll say the sounds in (pause) **hot** the hard way. Listen.
                                H (pause) **ooo** (pause) **t**.
b. Your turn. Say the sounds in (pause) **hot**. Get ready. Signal for
    each sound as the children say *h* (pause) *ooo* (pause) *t*. The children
    are to pause two seconds between the sounds. Repeat until firm.
c. Everybody, write the word (pause) **hot**. Check children's
                                                responses.

TASK 3   Children write rim

a. You're going to write the word **rim**. Listen. **Rim**. Saying the
    sounds in (pause) **rim** the hard way. Get ready. Signal for each
    sound as the children say *rrr* (pause) *iii* (pause) *mmm*. The children
    are to pause two seconds between the sounds. Repeat until firm.
b. Everybody, write the word (pause) **rim**. Check children's responses.

TASK 4   Children write him

a. You're going to write the word (pause) **him**. This word is tough.
    I'll say the sounds in (pause) **him** the hard way. Listen.
                                H (pause) **iii** (pause) **mmm**.
b. Your turn. Say the sounds in (pause) **him**. Get ready.
    Signal for each sound as the children say *h* (pause) *iii* (pause) *mmm*.
    The children are to pause two seconds between the sounds.
                                                Repeat until firm.
c. Everybody, write the word (pause) **him**. Check children's
                                                responses.

END OF SPELLING LESSON

Spelling Lesson 43

SOUND WRITING

TASK 1   Children write u

a. You're going to write a sound.
b. Here's the sound you're going to write. Listen. **uuu**.
                                What sound? (Signal.) *uuu*.
c. Write **uuu**. Check children's responses.

WORD WRITING

TASK 2 Children write **sam**, **ham**, **not**, **hit**, **hat**

a. You're going to write the word **sam**. Think about the sounds in (pause) **sam** and write the word. Check children's responses.

To correct	1. Say the sounds in **sam**. (Signal.) *Sssaaammm.*
	2. Say the sounds the hard way. (Signal.) *Sss* (pause) *aaa* (pause) *mmm.*
	3. Write the word **sam**. Check children's responses.

b. Repeat *a* for the following: **ham**, **not**, **hit**, **hat**.

TASK 3 Children write **him**

a. You're going to write the word (pause) **him**. This word is tough. I'll say the sounds in (pause) **him** the hard way. Listen. **H** (pause) **iii** (pause) **mmm**.
b. Your turn. Say the sounds in (pause) **him**. Get ready. Signal for each sound as the children say *h* (pause) *iii* (pause) *mmm.* The children are to pause two seconds between the sounds. Repeat until firm.
c. Everybody, write the word (pause) **him**. Check children's responses.

TASK 4 Children write **on**, **if**

a. You're going to write the word **on**. Think about the sounds in (pause) **on** and write the word. Check children's responses.
b. Repeat *a* for **if**.

END OF SPELLING LESSON

Spelling Lesson 44

SOUND WRITING

TASK 1 Children write **u**

a. You're going to write a sound.
b. Here's the sound you're going to write. Listen. **uuu**. What sound? (Signal.) *uuu.*
c. Write **uuu**. Check children's responses.

WORD WRITING

TASK 2 Children write **him**

a. You're going to write the word (pause) **him**. This word is tough. I'll say the sounds in (pause) **him** the hard way. Listen. **H** (pause) **iii** (pause) **mmm**.
b. Your turn. Say the sounds in (pause) **him**. Get ready. Signal for each sound as the children say *h* (pause) *iii* (pause) *mmm.* The children are to pause two seconds between the sounds. Repeat until firm.
c. Everybody, write the word (pause) **him**. Check children's responses.

TASK 3 Children write **sun**

a. You're going to write the word **sun**. Listen. **Sun**. Saying the sounds in (pause) **sun** the hard way. Get ready. Signal for each sound as the children say *sss* (pause) *uuu* (pause) *nnn.* The children are to pause two seconds between the sounds. Repeat until firm.
b. Everybody, write the word (pause) **sun**. Check children's responses.

TASK 4   Children write not

You're going to write the word **not**. Think about the sounds in
(pause) **not** and write the word. Check children's responses.

To correct	1. Say the sounds in **not**. (Signal.) *Nnnooot*. 2. Say the sounds the hard way. (Signal.) *Nnn* (pause) *ooo* (pause) *t*. 3. Write the word **not**. Check children's responses.

TASK 5   Children write nut

a. You're going to write the word **nut**. Listen. **Nut**. Saying the sounds in (pause) **nut** the hard way. Get ready. Signal for each sound as the children say *nnn* (pause) *uuu* (pause) *t*. The children are to pause two seconds between the sounds. Repeat until firm.
b. Everybody, write the word (pause) **nut**. Check children's responses.

TASK 6   Children write ron

You're going to write the word **ron**. Think about the sounds in
(pause) **ron** and write the word. Check children's responses.

TASK 7   Children write run, fun

a. You're going to write the word **run**. Listen. **Run**. Saying the sounds in (pause) **run** the hard way. Get ready. Signal for each sound as the children say *rrr* (pause) *uuu* (pause) *nnn*. The children are to pause two seconds between the sounds. Repeat until firm.
b. Everybody, write the word (pause) **run**. Check children's responses.
c. Repeat *a* and *b* for **fun**.

TASK 8   Children write if

a. You're going to write the word **if**. Think about the sounds in
(pause) **if** and write the word. Check children's responses.

Spelling Lesson 45

WORD WRITING

TASK 1   Children write fun

a. You're going to write the word **fun**. Listen. **Fun**. Saying the sounds in (pause) **fun** the hard way. Get ready. Signal for each sound as the children say *fff* (pause) *uuu* (pause) *nnn*. The children are to pause two seconds between the sounds. Repeat until firm.
b. Everybody, write the word (pause) **fun**. Check children's responses.

TASK 2   Children write fin, on, am

a. You're going to write the word **fin**. Think about the sounds in
(pause) **fin** and write the word. Check children's responses.

To correct	1. Say the sounds in **fin**. (Signal.) *Fffiiinnn*. 2. Say the sounds the hard way. (Signal.) *Fff* (pause) *iii* (pause) *nnn*. 3. Write the word **fin**. Check children's responses.

b. Repeat *a* for **on** and **am**.

TASK 3   Children write his

a. You're going to write the word (pause) **his**. Say the sounds you write for (pause) **his**. Get ready. Signal for each sound as the children say *h* (pause) *iii* (pause) *sss*. The children are to pause two seconds between the sounds. Repeat until firm.
b. Everybody, write the word (pause) **his**. Check children's responses.

TASK 4   Children write hot

You're going to write the word **hot**. Think about the sounds in (pause) **hot** and write the word. Check children's responses.

END OF SPELLING LESSON

TASK 5   Children write nut

a. You're going to write the word **nut**. Listen. **Nut**. Saying the sounds in (pause) **nut** the hard way. Get ready. Signal for each sound as the children say *nnn* (pause) *uuu* (pause) *t.* The children are to pause two seconds between the sounds. Repeat until firm.

b. Everybody, write the word (pause) **nut**. Check children's responses.

END OF SPELLING LESSON

Spelling Lesson 46

WORD WRITING

TASK 1   Children write ran

You're going to write the word **ran**. Think about the sounds in (pause) **ran** and write the word. Check children's responses.

To correct	1. Say the sounds in **ran**. (Signal.) *Rrraaannn.*
	2. Say the sounds the hard way. (Signal.) *Rrr* (pause) *aaa* (pause) *nnn.*
	3. Write the word **ran**. Check children's responses.

TASK 2   Children write run

a. You're going to write the word **run**. Listen. **Run**. Saying the sounds in (pause) **run** the hard way. Get ready. Signal for each sound as the children say *rrr* (pause) *uuu* (pause) *nnn.* The children are to pause two seconds between the sounds. Repeat until firm.

b. Everybody, write the word (pause) **run**. Check children's responses.

TASK 3   Children write sit, sun, hot

a. You're going to write the word **sit**. Think about the sounds in (pause) **sit** and write the word. Check children's responses.

b. Repeat *a* for **sun** and **hot**.

TASK 4   Children write hut

a. You're going to write the word **hut**. Listen. **Hut**. Saying the sounds in (pause) **hut** the hard way. Get ready. Signal for each sound as the children say *h* (pause) *uuu* (pause) *t.* The children are to pause two seconds between the sounds. Repeat until firm.

b. Everybody, write the word (pause) **hut**. Check children's responses.

TASK 5   Children write hit

You're going to write the word **hit**. Think about the sounds in (pause) **hit** and write the word. Check children's responses.

END OF SPELLING LESSON

Spelling Lesson 47

WORD WRITING

TASK 1   Children write hum

a. You're going to write the word (pause) **hum**. This word is tough. I'll say the sounds in (pause) **hum** the hard way. Listen. **H** (pause) **uuu** (pause) **mmm**.

b. Your turn. Say the sounds in (pause) **hum**. Get ready. Signal for each sound as the children say *h* (pause) *uuu* (pause) *mmm.* The children are to pause two seconds between the sounds. Repeat until firm.

c. Everybody, write the word (pause) **hum**. Check children's responses.

TASK 2   Children write him, ham

a. You're going to write the word **him**. Think about the sounds in (pause) **him** and write the word. Check children's responses.

To correct	1. Say the sounds in **him**. (Signal.) *Hiiimmm.*
	2. Say the sounds the hard way. (Signal.) *H* (pause) *iii* (pause) *mmm.*
	3. Write the word **him**. Check children's responses.

b. Repeat *a* for **ham**.

TASK 3   Children write has

a. You're going to write the word (pause) **has**. Say the sounds you write for (pause) **has**. Get ready. Signal for each sound as the children say *h* (pause) *aaa* (pause) *sss*. The children are to pause two seconds between the sounds. Repeat until firm.

b. Everybody, write the word (pause) **has**. Check children's responses.

TASK 4   Children write not, nut, rut, on

a. You're going to write the word **not**. Think about the sounds in (pause) **not** and write the word. Check children's responses.

b. Repeat *a* for **nut, rut**, and **on**.

END OF SPELLING LESSON

Spelling Lesson 48

WORD WRITING

TASK   Children write fit, on, rat, his, has, mat, run, sit

a. You're going to write the word **fit**. Think about the sounds in (pause) **fit** and write the word. Check children's responses.

To correct	1. Say the sounds in **fit**. (Signal.) *Fffiiit*. 2. Say the sounds the hard way. (Signal.) *Fff* (pause) *iii* (pause) *t*. 3. Write the word **fit**. Check children's responses.

b. Repeat *a* for **on** and **rat**.

c. You're going to write the word **his**. Think about the sounds in (pause) **his** and write the word. Check children's responses.

To correct	1. Say the sounds the hard way. (Signal.) *H* (pause) *iii* (pause) *sss*. 2. Write the word **his**. Check children's responses.

d. Repeat *c* for **has**.

e. Repeat *a* for **mat, run**, and **sit**.

END OF SPELLING LESSON

Spelling Lesson 49

WORD WRITING

TASK   Children write fat, run, is, fan, hut, hat, fun, hot

a. You're going to write the word **fat**. Think about the sounds in (pause) **fat** and write the word. Check children's responses.

To correct	1. Say the sounds in **fat**. (Signal.) *Fffaaat*. 2. Say the sounds the hard way. (Signal.) *Fff* (pause) *aaa* (pause) *t*. 3. Write the word **fat**. Check children's responses.

b. Repeat *a* for **run**.

c. You're going to write the word **is**. Think about the sounds in (pause) **is** and write the word. Check children's responses.

To correct	1. Say the sounds the hard way. (Signal.) *Iii* (pause) *sss*. 2. Write the word **is**. Check children's responses.

d. Repeat *a* for the following: **fan, hut, hat, fun, hot**.

END OF SPELLING LESSON

Spelling Lesson 50

WORD WRITING

TASK   Children write fun, if, not, run, sit, ran, sat, fan

a. You're going to write the word **fun**. Think about the sounds in (pause) **fun** and write the word. Check children's responses.

To correct	1. Say the sounds in **fun**. (Signal.) *Fffuuunnn*. 2. Say the sounds the hard way. (Signal.) *Fff* (pause) *uuu* (pause) *nnn*. 3. Write the word **fun**. Check children's responses.

b. Repeat *a* for the following: **if, not, run, sit, ran, sat, fan**.

END OF SPELLING LESSON

Spelling Lesson 51

WORD WRITING

TASK   Children write **ham, nut, fat, hot, fun, hit, on, has**

a. You're going to write the word **ham.** Think about the sounds in (pause) **ham** and write the word. Check children's responses.

To correct	1. Say the sounds in **ham.** (Signal.) *Haaammm.* 2. Say the sounds the hard way. (Signal.) *H* (pause) *aaa* (pause) *mmm.* 3. Write the word **ham.** Check children's responses.

b. Repeat *a* for the following: **nut, fat, hot, fun, hit, on.**

c. You're going to write the word **has.** Think about the sounds in (pause) **has** and write the word. Check children's responses.

To correct	1. Say the sounds the hard way. (Signal.) *H* (pause) *aaa* (pause) *sss.* 2. Write the word **has.** Check children's responses.

END OF SPELLING LESSON

Spelling Lesson 52

WORD WRITING

TASK   Children write **rat, ran, fit, sun, rut, an, fin, hut**

a. You're going to write the word **rat.** Think about the sounds in (pause) **rat** and write the word. Check children's responses.

To correct	1. Say the sounds in **rat.** (Signal.) *Rrraaat.* 2. Say the sounds the hard way. (Signal.) *Rrr* (pause) *aaa* (pause) *t.* 3. Write the word **rat.** Check children's responses.

b. Repeat *a* for the following: **ran, fit, sun, rut, an, fin, hut.**

END OF SPELLING LESSON

Spelling Lesson 53

WORD WRITING

TASK   Children write **him, ham, hot, if, am, hum, not, on**

a. You're going to write the word **him.** Think about the sounds in (pause) **him** and write the word. Check children's responses.

To correct	1. Say the sounds in **him.** (Signal.) *Hiiimmm.* 2. Say the sounds the hard way. (Signal.) *H* (pause) *iii* (pause) *mmm.* 3. Write the word **him.** Check children's responses.

b. Repeat *a* for the following: **ham, hot, if, am, hum, not, on.**

END OF SPELLING LESSON

Spelling Lesson 54

SOUND WRITING

TASK 1   Children write **d**

a. You're going to write a sound.
b. Here's the sound you're going to write. Listen. **d.**
    What sound? (Signal.) *d.*
c. Write **d.** Check children's responses.

WORD WRITING

TASK 2   Children write **is, an, run, mat, in, rut, on, hat**

a. You're going to write the word **is.** Think about the sounds in (pause) **is** and write the word. Check children's responses.

To correct	1. Say the sounds the hard way. (Signal.) *Iii* (pause) *sss.* 2. Write the word **is.** Check children's responses.

TURN THE PAGE FOR THE REST OF TASK 2.

b. You're going to write the word **an**. Think about the sounds in (pause) **an** and write the word. Check children's responses.

To correct	1. Say the sounds in **an**. (Signal.) *Aaannn.*
	2. Say the sounds the hard way. (Signal.) *Aaa* (pause) *nnn.*
	3. Write the word **an**. Check children's responses.

c. Repeat *b* for the following: **run, mat, in, rut, on, hat.**

END OF SPELLING LESSON

Spelling Lesson 55

SOUND WRITING

TASK 1   Children write **d**

a. You're going to write a sound.

b. Here's the sound you're going to write. Listen. **d.**
What sound? (Signal.) *d.*

c. Write **d**. Check children's responses.

WORD WRITING

TASK 2   Children write **has, mat**

a. You're going to write the word **has**. Think about the sounds in (pause) **has** and write the word. Check children's responses.

| To correct | 1. Say the sounds the hard way. (Signal.) *H* (pause) *aaa* (pause) *sss.* |
| | 2. Write the word **has**. Check children's responses. |

b. Now you're going to write the word **mat**. Think about the sounds in (pause) **mat** and write the word. Check children's responses.

To correct	1. Say the sounds in **mat**. (Signal.) *Mmmaaat.*
	2. Say the sounds the hard way. (Signal.) *Mmm* (pause) *aaa* (pause) *t.*
	3. Write the word **mat**. Check children's responses.

TASK 3   Children write **mad**

a. You're going to write the word **mad**. Listen. **Mad.** Saying the sounds in (pause) **mad** the hard way. Get ready. Signal for each sound as the children say *mmm* (pause) *aaa* (pause) *d.* The children are to pause two seconds between the sounds. Repeat until firm.

b. Everybody, write the word (pause) **mad**. Check responses.

TASK 4   Children write **if**

You're going to write the word **if**. Think about the sounds in (pause) **if** and write the word. Check children's responses.

TASK 5   Children write **sad**

a. You're going to write the word **sad**. Listen. **Sad.** Saying the sounds in (pause) **sad** the hard way. Get ready. Signal for each sound as the children say *sss* (pause) *aaa* (pause) *d.* The children are to pause two seconds between the sounds. Repeat until firm.

b. Everybody, write the word (pause) **sad**. Check responses.

TASK 6   Children write **had**

a. You're going to write the word (pause) **had**. This word is tough. I'll say the sounds in (pause) **had** the hard way. Listen. **H** (pause one second) **aaa** (pause one second) **d**.

b. Your turn. Say the sounds in (pause) **had**. Get ready. Signal for each sound as the children say *h* (pause) *aaa* (pause) *d.* The children are to pause two seconds between the sounds. Repeat until firm.

c. Everybody, write the word (pause) **had**. Check children's responses.

TASK 7   Children write **hot, nut**

a. You're going to write the word **hot**. Think about the sounds in (pause) **hot** and write the word. Check children's responses.

b. Repeat *a* for **nut**.

END OF SPELLING LESSON

Spelling Lesson 56

WORD WRITING

TASK 1   Children write **mad**, **mud**, **sad**

a. You're going to write the word **mad**. Listen. **Mad**. Saying the sounds in (pause) **mad** the hard way. Get ready. Signal for each sound as the children say *mmm* (pause) *aaa* (pause) *d*. The children are to pause two seconds between the sounds. Repeat until firm.

b. Everybody, write the word (pause) **mad**. Check children's responses.

c. Repeat *a* and *b* for **mud** and **sad**.

TASK 2   Children write **mat**, **on**

a. You're going to write the word **mat**. Think about the sounds in (pause) **mat** and write the word. Check children's responses.

To correct	1. Say the sounds in **mat**. (Signal.) *Mmmaaat*.
	2. Say the sounds the hard way. (Signal.) *Mmm* (pause) *aaa* (pause) *t*.
	3. Write the word **mat**. Check children's responses.

b. Repeat *a* for **on**.

TASK 3   Children write **had**

a. You're going to write the word (pause) **had**. This word is tough. I'll say the sounds in (pause) **had** the hard way. Listen. **H** (pause one second) **aaa** (pause one second) **d**.

b. Your turn. Say the sounds in (pause) **had**. Get ready. Signal for each sound as the children say *h* (pause) *aaa* (pause) *d*. The children are to pause two seconds between the sounds. Repeat until firm.

c. Everybody, write the word (pause) **had**. Check children's responses.

TASK 4   Children write **sit**

You're going to write the word **sit**. Think about the sounds in (pause) **sit** and write the word. Check children's responses.

END OF SPELLING LESSON

Spelling Lesson 57

WORD WRITING

TASK 1   Children write **hot**, **sad**

a. You're going to write the word **hot**. Think about the sounds in (pause) **hot** and write the word. Check children's responses.

To correct	1. Say the sounds in **hot**. (Signal.) *Hooot*.
	2. Say the sounds the hard way. (Signal.) *H* (pause) *ooo* (pause) *t*.
	3. Write the word **hot**. Check children's responses.

b. Repeat *a* for **sad**.

TASK 2   Children write **nod**

a. You're going to write the word **nod**. Listen. **Nod**. Saying the sounds in (pause) **nod** the hard way. Get ready. Signal for each sound as the children say *nnn* (pause) *ooo* (pause) *d*. The children are to pause two seconds between the sounds. Repeat until firm.

b. Everybody, write the word (pause) **nod**. Check children's responses.

TASK 3   Children write **hum**, **his**, **him**, **nut**, **has**

a. You're going to write the word **hum**. Think about the sounds in (pause) **hum** and write the word. Check children's responses.

b. You're going to write the word **his**. Think about the sounds in (pause) **his** and write the word. Check children's responses.

| To correct | 1. Say the sounds the hard way. (Signal.) *H* (pause) *iii* (pause) *sss*. |
| | 2. Write the word **his**. Check children's responses. |

c. Repeat *a* for **him** and **nut**.

d. Repeat *b* for **has**.

END OF SPELLING LESSON

Spelling Lesson 58

WORD WRITING

TASK 1   Children write **sad**, **sun**

a. You're going to write the word **sad**. Think about the sounds in (pause) **sad** and write the word. Check children's responses.

To correct	1. Say the sounds in **sad**. (Signal.) *Sssaaad.*
	2. Say the sounds the hard way. (Signal.) *Sss* (pause) *aaa* (pause) *d.*
	3. Write the word **sad**. Check children's responses.

b. Repeat *a* for **sun**.

TASK 2   Children write **rid**

a. You're going to write the word **rid**. Listen. **Rid**. Saying the sounds in (pause) **rid** the hard way. Get ready. Signal for each sound as the children say *rrr* (pause) *iii* (pause) *d.* The children are to pause two seconds between the sounds. Repeat until firm.

b. Everybody, write the word (pause) **rid**. Check children's responses.

TASK 3   Children write **run**, **mad**, **it**, **mud**, **sit**

a. You're going to write the word **run**. Think about the sounds in (pause) **run** and write the word. Check children's responses.

b. Repeat *a* for the following: **mad**, **it**, **mud**, **sit**.

END OF SPELLING LESSON

Spelling Lesson 59

WORD WRITING

TASK 1   Children write **an**, **ran**

a. You're going to write the word **an**. Think about the sounds in (pause) **an** and write the word. Check children's responses.

To correct	1. Say the sounds in **an**. (Signal.) *Aaannn.*
	2. Say the sounds the hard way. (Signal.) *Aaa* (pause) *nnn.*
	3. Write the word **an**. Check children's responses.

b. Repeat *a* for **ran**.

TASK 2   Children write **dan**, **tan**

a. You're going to write the word (pause) **dan**. This word is tough. I'll say the sounds in (pause) **dan** the hard way. Listen. **D** (pause) **aaa** (pause) **nnn**.

b. Your turn. Say the sounds in (pause) **dan**. Get ready. Signal for each sound as the children say *d* (pause) *aaa* (pause) *nnn.* The children are to pause two seconds between sounds. Repeat until firm.

c. Everybody, write the word (pause) **dan**. Check children's responses.

d. Now you're going to write the word (pause) **tan**. This word is tough. I'll say the sounds in (pause) **tan** the hard way. Listen. **T** (pause) **aaa** (pause) **nnn**.

e. Your turn. Say the sounds in (pause) **tan**. Get ready. Signal for each sound as the children say *t* (pause) *aaa* (pause) *nnn.* The children are to pause two seconds between sounds. Repeat until firm.

f. Everybody, write the word (pause) **tan**. Check children's responses.

TASK 3   Children write **sun**, **fin**, **nut**, **mud**

a. You're going to write the word **sun**. Think about the sounds in (pause) **sun** and write the word. Check children's responses.

b. Repeat *a* for **fin**, **nut**, and **mud**.

END OF SPELLING LESSON

Spelling Lesson 60

WORD WRITING

TASK 1   Children write **mud**

You're going to write the word **mud**. Think about the sounds in (pause) **mud** and write the word.   Check children's responses.

To correct	1. Say the sounds in **mud**. (Signal.) *Mmmuuud.*
	2. Say the sounds the hard way. (Signal.) *Mmm* (pause) *uuu* (pause) *d.*
	3. Write the word **mud**. Check children's responses.

TASK 2   Children write **tan**

a. You're going to write the word (pause) **tan**. This word is tough. I'll say the sounds in (pause) **tan** the hard way. Listen. **T** (pause) **aaa** (pause) **nnn**.

b. Your turn. Say the sounds in (pause) **tan**. Get ready. Signal for each sound as the children say t (pause) aaa (pause) nnn. The children are to pause two seconds between sounds. Repeat until firm.

c. Everybody, write the word (pause) **tan**. Check children's responses.

TASK 3   Children write **not, fin, hat, fat, his, him**

a. You're going to write the word **not**. Think about the sounds in (pause) **not** and write the word.   Check children's responses.

b. Repeat a for **fin, hat,** and **fat.**

c. You're going to write the word **his**. Think about the sounds in (pause) **his** and write the word.   Check children's responses.

| To correct | 1. Say the sounds the hard way. (Signal.) *H* (pause) *iii* (pause) *sss.* |
| | 2. Write the word **his**. Check children's responses. |

d. Repeat a for **him.**

Spelling Lesson 61

SOUND WRITING

TASK 1   Children write **ē**

a. You're going to write a sound.

b. Here's the sound you're going to write. Listen. **ēēē**.
What sound? (Signal.) *ēēē*.

c. Write **ēēē**. Check children's responses.

WORD WRITING

TASK 2   Children write **ron, an**

a. You're going to write the word **ron**. Think about the sounds in (pause) **ron** and write the word.   Check children's responses.

To correct	1. Say the sounds in **ron**. (Signal.) *Rrrooonnn.*
	2. Say the sounds the hard way. (Signal.) *Rrr* (pause) *ooo* (pause) *nnn.*
	3. Write the word **ron**. Check children's responses.

b. Repeat a for **an.**

TASK 3   Children write **and**

a. You're going to write the word **and**. Listen. **And**. Saying the sounds in (pause) **and** the hard way. Get ready. Signal for each sound as the children say aaa (pause) nnn (pause) d. The children are to pause two seconds between the sounds. Repeat until firm.

b. Everybody, write the word (pause) **and**. Check children's responses.

TASK 4   Children write **hit**

You're going to write the word **hit**. Think about the sounds in (pause) **hit** and write the word.   Check children's responses.

END OF SPELLING LESSON

35

TASK 5   Children write tan

a. You're going to write the word (pause) **tan**. This word is tough.
   I'll say the sounds in (pause) **tan** the hard way. Listen.
   T (pause) **aaa** (pause) **nnn**.

b. Your turn. Say the sounds in (pause) **tan**. Get ready.
   Signal for each sound as the children say *t* (pause) *aaa* (pause)
   nnn. The children are to pause two seconds between the sounds.
                                                              Repeat until firm.

c. Everybody, write the word (pause) **tan**. Check responses.

TASK 6   Children write sit, his

a. You're going to write the word **sit**. Think about the sounds in
   (pause) **sit** and write the word. Check children's responses.

b. Repeat *a* for **his**.

END OF SPELLING LESSON

Spelling Lesson 62

SOUND WRITING

TASK 1   Children write ē

a. You're going to write a sound.
b. Here's the sound you're going to write. Listen. **ēēē**.
                                        What sound? (Signal.) *ēēē*.
c. Write **ēēē**. Check children's responses.

WORD WRITING

TASK 2   Children write me

a. You're going to write the word **me**. Listen. **Me**. Saying the sounds
   in (pause) **me** the hard way. Get ready. Signal for each sound
   as the children say *mmm* (pause) *ēēē*. The children are to pause
   two seconds between the sounds. Repeat until firm.
b. Everybody, write the word (pause) **me**. Check children's
                                                         responses.

TASK 3   Children write he

a. You're going to write the word (pause) **he**. This word is tough.
   I'll say the sounds in (pause) **he** the hard way. Listen.
   H (pause one second) **ēēē**.

b. Your turn. Say the sounds in (pause) **he**. Get ready. Signal for
   each sound as the children say *h* (pause) *ēēē*. The children are
   to pause two seconds between the sounds. Repeat until firm.

c. Everybody, write the word (pause) **he**. Check responses.

TASK 4   Children write ham

You're going to write the word **ham**. Think about the sounds in
   (pause) **ham** and write the word. Check children's responses.

TASK 5   Children write and

a. You're going to write the word **and**. Listen. **And**. Saying the
   sounds in (pause) **and** the hard way. Get ready. Signal for each
   sound as the children say *aaa* (pause) *nnn* (pause) *d*. The children
   are to pause two seconds between the sounds. Repeat until firm.
b. Everybody, write the word (pause) **and**. Check responses.

TASK 6   Children write hand

a. You're going to write the word (pause) **hand**. This word is tough.
   I'll say the sounds in (pause) **hand** the hard way. Listen.
   H (pause) **aaa** (pause) **nnn** (pause) **d**.

b. Your turn. Say the sounds in (pause) **hand**. Get ready.
   Signal for each sound as the children say *h* (pause) *aaa* (pause)
   nnn (pause) *d*. The children are to pause two seconds between
                                        sounds. Repeat until firm.

c. Everybody, write the word (pause) **hand**. Check responses.

TASK 7   Children write mud, fit

a. You're going to write the word **mud**. Think about the sounds in
   (pause) **mud** and write the word. Check children's responses.
b. Repeat *a* for **fit**.

END OF SPELLING LESSON

Spelling Lesson 63

WORD WRITING

TASK 1   Children write **me**

a. You're going to write the word **me**. Listen. **Me**. Saying the sounds in (pause) **me** the hard way. Get ready. Signal for each sound as the children say *mmm* (pause) *ēēē*. The children are to pause two seconds between the sounds. Repeat until firm.

b. Everybody, write the word (pause) **me**. Check responses.

TASK 2   Children write **he**

a. You're going to write the word (pause) **he**. This word is tough. I'll say the sounds in (pause) **he** the hard way. Listen. **H** (pause one second) *ēēē*.

b. Your turn. Say the sounds in (pause) **he**. Get ready. Signal for each sound as the children say *h* (pause) *eee*. The children are to pause two seconds between the sounds. Repeat until firm.

c. Everybody, write the word (pause) **he**. Check children's responses.

TASK 3   Children write **tan, fit**

a. You're going to write the word **tan**. Think about the sounds in (pause) **tan** and write the word. Check children's responses.

To correct	1. Say the sounds in **tan**. (Signal.) *Taaannn*.
	2. Say the sounds the hard way. (Signal.) *T* (pause) *aaa* (pause) *nnn*.
	3. Write the word **tan**. Check children's responses.

b. Repeat *a* for **fit**.

TASK 4   Children write **and**

a. You're going to write the word **and**. Listen. **And**. Saying the sounds in (pause) **and** the hard way. Get ready. Signal for each sound as the children say *aaa* (pause) *nnn* (pause) *d*. The children are to pause two seconds between the sounds. Repeat until firm.

b. Everybody, write the word (pause) **and**. Check responses.

TASK 5   Children write **hand**

a. You're going to write the word (pause) **hand**. This word is tough. I'll say the sounds in (pause) **hand** the hard way. Listen. **H** (pause) **aaa** (pause) **nnn** (pause) **d**.

b. Your turn. Say the sounds in (pause) **hand**. Get ready. Signal for each sound as the children say *h* (pause) *aaa* (pause) *nnn* (pause) *d*. The children are to pause two seconds between the sounds. Repeat until firm.

c. Everybody, write the word (pause) **hand**. Check responses.

TASK 6   Children write **fan, sin**

a. You're going to write the word **fan**. Think about the sounds in (pause) **fan** and write the word. Check children's responses.

b. Repeat *a* for **sin**.

END OF SPELLING LESSON

Spelling Lesson 64

SOUND WRITING

TASK 1   Children write **w**

a. You're going to write a sound.

b. Here's the sound you're going to write. Listen. **www**. What sound? (Signal.) *www*.

c. Write **www**. Check children's responses.

WORD WRITING

TASK 2   Children write **he**

a. You're going to write the word **he**. Listen. **He**. Saying the sounds in (pause) **he** the hard way. Get ready. Signal for each sound as the children say *h* (pause) *ēēē*. The children are to pause two seconds between the sounds. Repeat until firm.

b. Everybody, write the word (pause) **he**. Check children's responses.

TASK 3   Children write hand

a. You're going to write the word (pause) **hand**. This word is tough. I'll say the sounds in (pause) **hand** the hard way. Listen. **H** (pause) **aaa** (pause) **nnn** (pause) **d**.

b. Your turn. Say the sounds in (pause) **hand**. Get ready. Signal for each sound as the children say *h* (pause) *aaa* (pause) *nnn* (pause) *d*. The children are to pause two seconds between the sounds. Repeat until firm.

c. Everybody, write the word (pause) **hand**. Check children's responses.

TASK 4   Children write me

a. You're going to write the word **me**. Listen. **Me**. Saying the sounds in (pause) **me** the hard way. Get ready. Signal for each sound as the children say *mmm* (pause) *ēēē*. The children are to pause two seconds between the sounds. Repeat until firm.

b. Everybody, write the word (pause) **me**. Check children's responses.

TASK 5   Children write tan, dan, in

a. You're going to write the word **tan**. Think about the sounds in **tan** and write the word. Check children's responses.

To correct	1. Say the sounds in **tan**. (Signal.) *Taaannn.*
	2. Say the sounds the hard way. (Signal.) *T* (pause) *aaa* (pause) *nnn*.
	3. Write the word **tan**. Check children's responses.

b. Repeat *a* for **dan** and **in**.

TASK 6   Children write tin

a. You're going to write the word (pause) **tin**. This word is tough. I'll say the sounds in (pause) **tin** the hard way. Listen. **T** (pause) **iii** (pause) **nnn**.

b. Your turn. Say the sounds in (pause) **tin**. Get ready. Signal for each sound as the children say *t* (pause) *iii* (pause) *nnn*. The children are to pause two seconds between the sounds. Repeat until firm.

c. Everybody, write the word (pause) **tin**. Check children's responses.

TASK 7   Children write has

You're going to write the word **has**. Think about the sounds in (pause) **has** and write the word. Check children's responses.

| To correct | 1. Say the sounds the hard way. (Signal.) *H* (pause) *aaa* (pause) *sss*. |
| | 2. Write the word **has**. Check children's responses. |

END OF SPELLING LESSON

Spelling Lesson 65

SOUND WRITING

TASK 1   Children write w

a. You're going to write a sound.

b. Here's the sound you're going to write. Listen. **www**. What sound? (Signal.) *www*.

c. Write **www**. Check children's responses.

WORD WRITING

TASK 2   Children write we, had

a. You're going to write the word **we**. Listen. **We**. Saying the sounds in (pause) **we** the hard way. Get ready. Signal for each sound as the children say *www* (pause) *ēēē*. The children are to pause two seconds between the sounds. Repeat until firm.

b. Everybody, write the word (pause) **we** Check children's responses.

c. Repeat *a* and *b* for **had**.

TASK 3 Children write **he**

You're going to write the word **he**. Think about the sounds in (pause) **he** and write the word. Check children's responses.

To correct	1. Say the sounds in **he**. (Signal.) *Hēēē*.
	2. Say the sounds the hard way. (Signal.) *H* (pause) *ēēē*.
	3. Write the word **he**. Check children's responses.

TASK 4 Children write **win**

a. You're going to write the word **win**. Listen. **Win**. Saying the sounds in (pause) **win** the hard way. Get ready. Signal for each sound as the children say *www* (pause) *iii* (pause) *nnn*. The children are to pause two seconds between the sounds. Repeat until firm.

b. Everybody, write the word (pause) **win**. Check children's responses.

TASK 5 Children write **fit**, **if**, **on**

a. You're going to write the word **fit**. Think about the sounds in (pause) **fit** and write the word. Check children's responses.

b. Repeat *a* for **if** and **on**.

END OF SPELLING LESSON

Spelling Lesson 66

WORD WRITING

TASK 1 Children write **dan**, **on**

a. You're going to write the word **dan**. Think about the sounds in (pause) **dan** and write the word. Check children's responses.

To correct	1. Say the sounds in **dan**. (Signal.) *Daaannn*.
	2. Say the sounds the hard way. (Signal.) *D* (pause) *aaa* (pause) *nnn*.
	3. Write the word **dan**. Check children's responses.

b. Repeat *a* for **on**.

TASK 2 Children write **we**

a. You're going to write the word **we**. Listen. **We**. Saying the sounds in (pause) **we** the hard way. Get ready. Signal for each sound as the children say *www* (pause) *ēēē*. The children are to pause two seconds between the sounds. Repeat until firm.

b. Everybody, write the word (pause) **we**. Check children's responses.

TASK 3 Children write **in**, **sun**, **he**, **it**, **at**

a. You're going to write the word **in**. Think about the sounds in (pause) **in** and write the word. Check children's responses.

b. Repeat *a* for the following: **sun, he, it, at.**

END OF SPELLING LESSON

Spelling Lesson 67

WORD WRITING

TASK Children write **we, an, at, if, is, and, has, his**

a. You're going to write the word **we**. Think about the sounds in (pause) **we** and write the word. Check children's responses.

To correct	1. Say the sounds in **we**. (Signal.) *Wwwēēē*.
	2. Say the sounds the hard way. (Signal.) *Www* (pause) *ēēē*.
	3. Write the word **we**. Check children's responses.

b. Repeat *a* for **an, at,** and **if**.

c. You're going to write the word **is**. Think about the sounds in (pause) **is** and write the word. Check children's responses.

| To correct | 1. Say the sounds the hard way. (Signal.) *Iii* (pause) *sss*. |
| | 2. Write the word **is**. Check children's responses. |

d. Repeat *a* for **and**.

e. Repeat *c* for **has** and **his**.

END OF SPELLING LESSON

Spelling Lesson 68

SOUND WRITING

TASK 1   Children write l as in land

a. You're going to write a sound.

b. Here's the sound you're going to write. Listen. *lll.*

What sound. (Signal.) *lll.*

c. Write **lll**. Check children's responses.

WORD WRITING

TASK 2   Children write he, tan, mad, we

a. You're going to write the word **he**. Think about the sounds in
(pause) **he** and write the word. Check children's responses.

To correct	1. Say the sounds in **he**. (Signal.) *Hēēē.*
	2. Say the sounds the hard way. (Signal.) *H* (pause) *ēēē.*
	3. Write the word **he**. Check children's responses.

b. Repeat *a* for **tan, mad** and **we**.

TASK 3   Children write land

a. You're going to write the word **land**. Listen. **Land**. Saying the
sounds in (pause) **land** the hard way. Get ready. Signal for
each sound as the children say *lll* (pause) *aaa* (pause) *nnn*
(pause) *d.* The children are to pause two seconds between the
sounds. Repeat until firm.

b. Everybody, write the word (pause) **land**. Check children's
responses.

TASK 4   Children write has, mud

a. You're going to write the word **has**. Think about the sounds in
(pause) **has** and write the word. Check children's responses.

| To correct | 1. Say the sounds the hard way. (Signal.) *H* (pause) *aaa* (pause) *sss.* |
| | 2. Write the word **has**. Check children's responses. |

b. Repeat *a* for **mud**.

END OF SPELLING LESSON

Spelling Lesson 69

SOUND WRITING

TASK 1   Children write l as in land

a. You're going to write a sound.

b. Here's the sound you're going to write. Listen. *lll.*

What sound? (Signal.) *lll.*

c. Write **lll**. Check children's responses.

WORD WRITING

TASK 2   Children write nod

a. You're going to write the word **nod**. Listen. **Nod**. Saying the
sounds in (pause) **nod** the hard way. Get ready. Signal for
each sound as the children say *nnn* (pause) *ooo* (pause) *d.*
The children are to pause two seconds between the sounds.
Repeat until firm.

b. Everybody, write the word (pause) **nod**. Check children's
responses.

TASK 3   Children write and, hand, land

a. You're going to write the word **and**. Think about the sounds in (pause) **and** and write the word. Check children's responses.

To correct	1. **Say the sounds in and.** (Signal.) *Aaannnd.*
	2. **Say the sounds the hard way.** (Signal.) *Aaa* (pause) *nnn* (pause) *d.*
	3. **Write the word and.** Check children's responses.

b. Repeat *a* for **hand** and **land**.

TASK 4   Children write rid, lid

a. You're going to write the word **rid**. Listen. **Rid**. Saying the sounds in (pause) **rid** the hard way. Get ready. Signal for each sound as the children say *rrr* (pause) *iii* (pause) *d.* The children are to pause two seconds between the sounds. Repeat until firm.

b. Everybody, write the word (pause) **rid**. Check children's responses.

c. Repeat *a* and *b* for **lid**.

TASK 5   Children write if

You're going to write the word **if**. Think about the sounds in (pause) **if** and write the word. Check children's responses.

END OF SPELLING LESSON

Spelling Lesson 70

WORD WRITING

TASK 1   Children write hand, we, land, me, has

a. You're going to write the word **hand**. Think about the sounds in (pause) **hand** and write the word. Check children's responses.

b. Repeat *a* for **we, land,** and **me**.

c. You're going to write the word **has**. Think about the sounds in (pause) **has** and write the word. Check children's responses.

| To correct | 1. **Say the sounds the hard way.** (Signal.) *H* (pause) *aaa* (pause) *sss.* |
| | 2. **Write the word has.** Check children's responses. |

TASK 2   Children write win

a. You're going to write the word **win**. Listen. **Win**. Saying the sounds in (pause) **win** the hard way. Get ready. Signal for each sound as the children say *www* (pause) *iii* (pause) *nnn*. The children are to pause two seconds between the sounds. Repeat until firm.

b. Everybody, write the word (pause) **win**. Check children's responses.

TASK 3   Children write sit, lit

a. You're going to write the word **sit**. Think about the sounds in (pause) **sit** and write the word. Check children's responses.

b. Repeat *a* for **lit**.

END OF SPELLING LESSON

Spelling Lesson 71

WORD WRITING

TASK   Children write hot, hand, mud, tan, dan, nut, if, land

a. You're going to write the word **hot**. Think about the sounds in (pause) **hot** and write the word. Check children's responses.

To correct	1. **Say the sounds in hot.** (Signal.) *Hooot.*
	2. **Say the sounds the hard way.** (Signal.) *H* (pause) *ooo* (pause) *t.*
	3. **Write the word hot.** Check children's responses.

b. Repeat *a* for the following: **hand, mud, tan, dan, nut, if, land.**

END OF SPELLING LESSON

Spelling Lesson 72

WORD WRITING

TASK   Children write **nod, fit, tan, dan, fin, tin, his**

a. You're going to write the word **nod**. Think about the sounds in (pause) **nod** and write the word. Check children's responses.

To correct	1. Say the sounds in **nod**. (Signal.) *Nnnoood.*
	2. Say the sounds the hard way. (Signal.) *Nnn* (pause) *ooo* (pause) *d.*
	3. Write the word **nod**. Check children's responses.

b. Repeat *a* for the following: **fit, tan, dan, fin, tin.**
c. You're going to write the word **his**. Think about the sounds in (pause) **his** and write the word. Check children's responses.

To correct	1. Say the sounds the hard way. (Signal.) *H* (pause) *iii* (pause) *sss.*
	2. Write the word **his**. Check children's responses.

END OF SPELLING LESSON

TASK 2   Children write **sin, tin, hand**

a. You're going to write the word **sin**. Think about the sounds in (pause) **sin** and write the word. Check children's responses.

To correct	1. Say the sounds in **sin**. (Signal.) *Sssiiinnn.*
	2. Say the sounds the hard way. (Signal.) *Sss* (pause) *iii* (pause) *nnn.*
	3. Write the word **sin**. Check children's responses.

b. Repeat *a* for **tin** and **hand**.

TASK 3   Children write **sand**

a. You're going to write the word **sand**. Listen. **Sand.** Saying the sounds in (pause) **sand** the hard way. Get ready. Signal for each sound as the children say *sss* (pause) *aaa* (pause) *nnn* (pause) *d.* The children are to pause two seconds between the sounds. Repeat until firm.
b. Everybody, write the word (pause) **sand**. Check children's responses.

END OF SPELLING LESSON

Spelling Lesson 73

WORD WRITING

TASK 1   Children write **did, rid, hid**

a. You're going to write the word **did**. Listen. **Did.** Saying the sounds in (pause) **did** the hard way. Get ready. Signal for each sound as the children say *d* (pause) *iii* (pause) *d.* The children are to pause two seconds between the sounds. Repeat until firm.
b. Everybody, write the word (pause) **did**. Check children's responses.
c. Repeat *a* and *b* for **rid** and **hid**.

Spelling Lesson 74

WORD WRITING

TASK 1   Children write **did, dad**

a. You're going to write **did**. Listen. **Did.** Saying the sounds in (pause) **did** the hard way. Get ready. Signal for each sound as the children say *d* (pause) *iii* (pause) *d.* The children are to pause two seconds between the sounds. Repeat until firm.
b. Everybody, write the word (pause) **did**. Check children's responses.
c. Repeat *a* and *b* for **dad.**

TASK 2   Children write **tin**

You're going to write the word **tin**. Think about the sounds in   (pause) **tin** and write the word.   Check children's responses.

To correct	1. Say the sounds in **tin**. (Signal.) *Tiiinnn.*
	2. Say the sounds the hard way. (Signal.) *T* (pause) *iii* (pause) *nnn.*
	3. Write the word **tin**. Check children's responses.

TASK 3   Children write **sand**

a. You're going to write the word **sand**. Listen. **Sand**. Saying the sounds in   (pause) **sand** the hard way. Get ready.   Signal for each sound as the children say *sss* (pause) *aaa* (pause) *nnn* (pause) *d.* The children are to pause two seconds between the sounds. Repeat until firm.

b. Everybody, write the word   (pause) **sand**. Check children's responses.

TASK 4   Children write **not**, **me**, **his**

a. You're going to write the word **not**. Think about the sounds in   (pause) **not** and write the word.   Check children's responses.

To correct	1. Say the sounds in **not**. (Signal.) *Nnnooot.*
	2. Say the sounds the hard way. (Signal.) *Nnn* (pause) *ooo* (pause) *t.*
	3. Write the word **not**. Check children's responses.

b. Repeat *a* for **me**.
c. You're going to write the word **his**. Think about the sounds in   (pause) **his** and write the word.   Check children's responses.

| To correct | 1. Say the sounds the hard way. (Signal.) *H* (pause) *iii* (pause) *sss.* |
| | 2. Write the word **his**. Check children's responses. |

END OF SPELLING LESSON

Spelling Lesson 75

WORD WRITING

TASK 1   Children write **sun**, **sit**, **he**, **sad**

a. You're going to write the word **sun**. Think about the sounds in   (pause) **sun** and write the word.   Check children's responses.

To correct	1. Say the sounds in **sun**. (Signal.) *Sssuuunnn.*
	2. Say the sounds the hard way. (Signal.) *Sss* (pause) *uuu* (pause) *nnn.*
	3. Write the word **sun**. Check children's responses.

b. Repeat *a* for **sit**, **he**, and **sad**.

TASK 2   Children write **dad**

a. You're going to write the word **dad**. Listen. **Dad**. Saying the sounds in   (pause) **dad** the hard way. Get ready.   Signal for each sound as the children say *d* (pause) *aaa* (pause) *d.* The children are to pause two seconds between the sounds. Repeat until firm.
b. Everybody, write the word   (pause) **dad**. Check children's responses.

TASK 3   Children write **had**, **ron**, **fit**

a. You're going to write the word **had**. Think about the sounds in   (pause) **had** and write the word.   Check children's responses.
b. Repeat *a* for **ron** and **fit**.

END OF SPELLING LESSON

Spelling Lesson 76

WORD WRITING

TASK 1   Children write **did**

a. You're going to write the word **did**. Listen. **Did**. Saying the sounds in (pause) **did** the hard way. Get ready. Signal for each sound as the children say *d* (pause) *iii* (pause) *d*. The children are to pause two seconds between the sounds. Repeat until firm.

b. Everybody, write the word (pause) **did**. Check children's responses.

TASK 2   Children write **land**, **not**

a. You're going to write the word **land**. Think about the sounds in (pause) **land** and write the word. Check children's responses.

To correct	1. Say the sounds in **land**. (Signal.) *Lllaaannnd*. 2. Say the sounds the hard way. (Signal.) *Lll* (pause) *aaa* (pause) *nnn* (pause) *d*. 3. Write the word **land**. Check children's responses.

b. Repeat *a* for **not**.

TASK 3   Children write **hid**

a. You're going to write the word **hid**. Listen. **Hid**. Saying the sounds in (pause) **hid** the hard way. Get ready. Signal for each sound as the children say *h* (pause) *iii* (pause) *d*. The children are to pause two seconds between the sounds. Repeat until firm.

b. Everybody, write the word (pause) **hid**. Check children's responses.

TASK 4   Children write **has**, **mud**, **hot**, **we**

a. You're going to write the word **has**. Think about the sounds in (pause) **has** and write the word. Check children's responses.

To correct	1. Say the sounds the hard way. (Signal.) *H* (pause) *aaa* (pause) *sss*. 2. Write the word **has**. Check children's responses.

b. You're going to write the word **mud**. Think about the sounds in (pause) **mud** and write the word. Check children's responses.

To correct	1. Say the sounds in **mud**. (Signal.) *Mmmuuud*. 2. Say the sounds the hard way. (Signal.) *Mmm* (pause) *uuu* (pause) *d*. 3. Write the word **mud**. Check children's responses.

c. Repeat *b* for **hot** and **we**.

END OF SPELLING LESSON

Spelling Lesson 77

WORD WRITING

TASK   Children write **and**, **land**, **sand**, **hand**, **if**, **has**, **is**, **on**

a. You're going to write the word **and**. Think about the sounds in (pause) **and** and write the word. Check children's responses.

To correct	1. Say the sounds in **and**. (Signal.) *Aaannnd*. 2. Say the sounds the hard way. (Signal.) *Aaa* (pause) *nnn* (pause) *d*. 3. Write the word **and**. Check children's responses.

b. Repeat *a* for the following: **land, sand, hand, if**.

c. You're going to write the word **has**. Think about the sounds in (pause) **has** and write the word. Check children's responses.

To correct	1. Say the sounds the hard way. (Signal.) *H* (pause) *aaa* (pause) *sss*. 2. Write the word **has**. Check children's responses.

d. Repeat *c* for **is**.

e. Repeat *a* for **on**.

END OF SPELLING LESSON

Spelling Lesson 78

WORD WRITING

TASK 1 Children write **me**

You're going to write the word **me**. Think about the sounds in (pause) **me** and write the word. Check children's responses.

To correct	1. Say the sounds in **me**. (Signal.) *Mmmēēē*.
	2. Say the sounds the hard way. (Signal.) *Mmm* (pause) *ēēē*.
	3. Write the word **me**. Check children's responses.

TASK 2 Children write **win**

a. You're going to write the word **win**. Listen. **Win**. Saying the sounds in (pause) **win** the hard way. Get ready. Signal for each sound as the children say *www* (pause) *iii* (pause) *nnn*. The children are to pause two seconds between the sounds. Repeat until firm.
b. Everybody, write the word (pause) **win**. Check children's responses.

TASK 3 Children write **and**

You're going to write the word **and**. Think about the sounds in (pause) **and** and write the word. Check children's responses.

TASK 4 Children write **ant**

a. You're going to write the word (pause) **ant**. Say the sounds you write for (pause) **ant**. Get ready. Signal for each sound as the children say *aaa* (pause) *nnn* (pause) *t*. The children are to pause two seconds between the sounds. Repeat until firm.
b. Everybody, write the word (pause) **ant**. Check children's responses.

TASK 5 Children write **we**, **sit**, **he**, **fat**

a. You're going to write the word **we**. Think about the sounds in (pause) **we** and write the word. Check children's responses.
b. Repeat a for **sit**, **he**, and **fat**.

END OF SPELLING LESSON

Spelling Lesson 79

WORD WRITING

TASK 1 Children write **me**, **has**

a. You're going to write the word **me**. Think about the sounds in (pause) **me** and write the word. Check children's responses.

To correct	1. Say the sounds in **me**. (Signal.) *Mmmēēē*.
	2. Say the sounds the hard way. (Signal.) *Mmm* (pause) *ēēē*.
	3. Write the word **me**. Check children's responses.

b. Now you're going to write the word **has**. Think about the sounds in (pause) **has** and write the word. Check children's responses.

| To correct | 1. Say the sounds the hard way. (Signal.) *H* (pause) *aaa* (pause) *sss*. |
| | 2. Write the word **has**. Check children's responses. |

TASK 2 Children write **was**

a. You're going to write the word (pause) **was**. When you write the word (pause) **was**, you write these sounds. **Www** (pause) **aaa** (pause) **sss**.
b. Say the sounds you write for (pause) **was**. Signal for each sound as the children say *www* (pause) *aaa* (pause) *sss*. The children are to pause two seconds between the sounds. Repeat until firm.
c. Everybody, write the word (pause) **was**. Check children's responses.

TASK 3   Children write we

You're going to write the word **we**. Think about the sounds in (pause) **we** and write the word. Check children's responses.

TASK 4   Children write dad

a. You're going to write the word **dad**. Listen. **Dad**. Saying the sounds in (pause) **dad** the hard way. Get ready. Signal for each sound as the children say *d* (pause) *aaa* (pause) *d*. The children are to pause two seconds between the sounds. Repeat until firm.
b. Everybody, write the word (pause) **dad**. Check children's responses.

TASK 5   Children write tin, an, ant

a. You're going to write the word **tin**. Think about the sounds in (pause) **tin** and write the word. Check children's responses.

To correct	1. Say the sounds in **tin**. (Signal.) *Tiiinnn*.
	2. Say the sounds the hard way. (Signal.) *T* (pause) *iii* (pause) *nnn*.
	3. Write the word **tin**. Check children's responses.

b. Repeat *a* for **an** and **ant**.

END OF SPELLING LESSON

Spelling Lesson 80

WORD WRITING

TASK 1   Children write we

a. You're going to write the word **we**. Think about the sounds in (pause) **we** and write the word. Check children's responses.

To correct	1. Say the sounds in **we**. (Signal.) *Wwwēēē*.
	2. Say the sounds the hard way. (Signal.) *Www* (pause) *ēēē*.
	3. Write the word **we**. Check children's responses.

b. Now you're going to write the word **has**. Think about the sounds in (pause) **has** and write the word. Check children's responses.

To correct	1. Say the sounds the hard way. (Signal.) *H* (pause) *aaa* (pause) *sss*.
	2. Write the word **has**. Check children's responses.

TASK 2   Children write was

a. You're going to write the word (pause) **was**. When you write the word (pause) **was**, you write these sounds. *Www* (pause) *aaa* (pause) *sss*.
b. Say the sounds you write for (pause) **was**. Signal for each sound as the children say *www* (pause) *aaa* (pause) *sss*. The children are to pause two seconds between sounds. Repeat until firm.
c. Everybody, write the word (pause) **was**. Check children's responses.

TASK 3   Children write tin, land, sand

a. You're going to write the word **tin**. Think about the sounds in (pause) **tin** and write the word. Check children's responses.
b. Repeat *a* for **land** and **sand**.

END OF SPELLING LESSON

Spelling Lesson 81

WORD WRITING

TASK 1   Children write has

You're going to write the word **has**. Think about the sounds in (pause) **has** and write the word. Check children's responses.

To correct	1. Say the sounds the hard way. (Signal.) *H* (pause) *aaa* (pause) *sss*.
	2. Write the word **has**. Check children's responses.

TASK 2 Children write **was**

a. You're going to write the word (pause) **was**. When you write the word (pause) **was**, you write these sounds. **Www** (pause) **aaa** (pause) **sss**.

b. Say the sounds you write for (pause) **was**. Signal for each sound as the children say *www* (pause) *aaa* (pause) *sss*. The children are to pause two seconds between sounds. Repeat until firm.

c. Everybody, write the word (pause) **was**. Check children's responses.

TASK 3 Children write **hid**, **did**, **dad**, **tin**

a. You're going to write the word **hid**. Think about the sounds in (pause) **hid** and write the word. Check children's responses.

To correct	1. Say the sounds in **hid**. *Hiiid.*
	2. Say the sounds the hard way. *H* (pause) *iii* (pause) *d.*
	3. Write the word **hid**. Check children's responses.

b. Repeat *a* for **did**, **dad**, and **tin**.

END OF SPELLING LESSON

Spelling Lesson 82

WORD WRITING

TASK 1 Children write **is**, **has**, **his**

a. You're going to write the word **is**. Think about the sounds in (pause) **is** and write the word. Check children's responses.

| To correct | 1. Say the sounds the hard way. (Signal.) *Iii* (pause) *sss.* |
| | 2. Write the word **is**. Check children's responses. |

b. Repeat *a* for **has** and **his**.

TASK 2 Children write **was**

a. You're going to write the word (pause) **was**. Say the sounds you write for (pause) **was**. Get ready. Signal for each sound as the children say *www* (pause) *aaa* (pause) *sss*. The children are to pause two seconds between the sounds. Repeat until firm.

b. Everybody, write the word (pause) **was**. Check children's responses.

SENTENCE WRITING

TASK 3 Children write a sentence

a. Listen to this sentence. **He hit me.** Your turn. Say that sentence. Get ready. (Signal.) *He hit me.*

b. Now you're going to say it the slow way. Get ready. Signal for each word as the children say *he* (pause) *hit* (pause) *me.* Repeat until firm.

c. Everybody, write the sentence. Spell each word the right way. As you check children's responses, remind the children: **Don't forget to put a period at the end of your sentence.**

END OF SPELLING LESSON

Spelling Lesson 83

SOUND WRITING

TASK 1 Children write **c**

a. You're going to write a sound.

b. Here's the sound you're going to write. Listen. **c**. What sound? (Signal.) *c.*

c. Write **c** on the board. Here's the **c** you're going to write. Then erase **c**.

d. Write **c**. Check children's responses.

WORD WRITING

TASK 2   Children write **was**

a. You're going to write the word (pause) **was**. Say the sounds you write for (pause) **was**. Get ready. Signal for each sound as the children say *www* (pause) *aaa* (pause) *sss*. The children are to pause two seconds between the sounds. Repeat until firm.
b. Everybody, write the word (pause) **was**. Check children's responses.

TASK 3   Children write **tin**, **did**, **we**

a. You're going to write the word **tin**. Think about the sounds in (pause) **tin** and write the word. Check children's responses.

To correct	1. Say the sounds in **tin**. (Signal.) *Tiiinnn.*
	2. Say the sounds the hard way. (Signal.) *T* (pause) *iii* (pause) *nnn.*
	3. Write the word **tin**. Check children's responses.

b. Repeat *a* for **did** and **we**.

SENTENCE WRITING

TASK 4   Children write a sentence

a. Listen to this sentence. **We had sand**. Your turn. Say that sentence. Get ready. (Signal.) *We had sand.*
b. Now you're going to say it the slow way. Get ready. Signal for each word as the children say *we* (pause) *had* (pause) *sand.* Repeat until firm.
c. Everybody, write the sentence. Spell each word the right way. As you check children's responses, remind the children: **Don't forget to put a period at the end of your sentence.**

END OF SPELLING LESSON

Spelling Lesson 84

SOUND WRITING

TASK 1   Children write **c**

a. You're going to write a sound.
b. Here's the sound you're going to write. Listen. **c**. What sound? (Signal.) *c*.
c. Write **c** on the board. Here's the **c** you're going to write. Then erase **c**.
d. Write **c**. Check children's responses.

WORD WRITING

TASK 2   Children write **can**

a. You're going to write the word (pause) **can**. This word is tough. I'll say the sounds in (pause) **can** the hard way. Listen. **C** (pause) **aaa** (pause) **nnn**.
b. Your turn. Say the sounds in (pause) **can**. Get ready. Signal for each sound as the children say *c* (pause) *aaa* (pause) *nnn*. The children are to pause two seconds between sounds. Repeat until firm.
c. Everybody, write the word (pause) **can**. Check children's responses.

TASK 3   Children write **has**

You're going to write the word **has**. Think about the sounds in (pause) **has** and write the word. Check children's responses.

| To correct | 1. Say the sounds the hard way. (Signal.) *H* (pause) *aaa* (pause) *sss.* |
| | 2. Write the word **has**. Check children's responses. |

TASK 4   Children write **was**

a. You're going to write the word (pause) **was**. Say the sounds you write for (pause) **was**. Get ready. Signal for each sound as the children say *www* (pause) *aaa* (pause) *sss*. The children are to pause two seconds between the sounds. Repeat until firm.
b. Everybody, write the word (pause) **was**. Check responses.

TASK 5　Children write land, nut

a. You're going to write the word **land**. Think about the sounds in (pause) **land** and write the word.　Check children's responses.

To correct	1. Say the sounds in **land**.　(Signal.) *Lllaaannnd*.
	2. Say the sounds the hard way.　(Signal.) *Lll* (pause) *aaa* (pause) *nnn* (pause) *d*.
	3. Write the word **land**.　Check children's responses.

b. Repeat *a* for **nut**.

SENTENCE WRITING

TASK 6　Children write a sentence

a. Listen to this sentence. **He had fun.** Your turn. Say that sentence. Get ready.　(Signal.) *He had fun.*

b. Now you're going to say it the slow way. Get ready.　Signal for each word as the children say *he* (pause) *had* (pause) *fun*. Repeat until firm.

c. Everybody, write the sentence. Spell each word the right way.　As you check children's responses, remind the children: **Don't forget to put a period at the end of your sentence.**

END OF SPELLING LESSON

Spelling Lesson 85

WORD WRITING

TASK 1　Children write can

a. You're going to write the word (pause) **can**. This word is tough. I'll say the sounds in (pause) **can** the hard way. Listen. **C** (pause) **aaa** (pause) **nnn**.

b. Your turn. Say the sounds in (pause) **can**. Get ready.　Signal for each sound as the children say *c* (pause) *aaa* (pause) *nnn*. The children are to pause two seconds between the sounds. Repeat until firm.

c. Everybody, write the word (pause) **can**.　Check responses.

TASK 2　Children write arm

a. You're going to write the word　(pause) **arm**. When you write the word　(pause) **arm**, you write these sounds. **Aaa** (pause) **rrr** (pause) **mmm**.

b. Say the sounds you write for　(pause) **arm**. Signal for each sound as the children say *aaa* (pause) *rrr* (pause) *mmm*. The children are to pause two seconds between the sounds. Repeat until firm.

c. Everybody, write the word　(pause) **arm**. Check children's responses.

TASK 3　Children write sand, fit, mud, tin

a. You're going to write the word **sand**. Think about the sounds in (pause) **sand** and write the word.　Check children's responses.

To correct	1. Say the sounds in **sand**.　(Signal.) *Sssaaannnd*.
	2. Say the sounds the hard way.　(Signal.) *Sss* (pause) *aaa* (pause) *nnn* (pause) *d*.
	3. Write the word **sand**.　Check children's responses.

b. Repeat *a* for **fit**, **mud**, and **tin**.

SENTENCE WRITING

TASK 4　Children write a sentence

a. Listen to this sentence. **He was mad**. Your turn. Say that sentence. Get ready.　(Signal.) *He was mad.*

b. Now you're going to say it the slow way. Get ready.　Signal for each word as the children say *he* (pause) *was* (pause) *mad*. Repeat until firm.

c. Everybody, write the sentence. Spell each word the right way.　As you check children's responses, remind the children: **Don't forget to put a period at the end of your sentence.**

END OF SPELLING LESSON

Spelling Lesson 86

WORD WRITING

TASK 1   Children write if, am

a. You're going to write the word **if**. Think about the sounds in (pause) **if** and write the word. Check children's responses.

To correct	**1.** Say the sounds in **if**. (Signal.) *Iiifff*. **2.** Say the sounds the hard way. (Signal.) *Iii* (pause) *fff*. **3.** Write the word **if**. Check children's responses.

b. Repeat *a* for **am**.

TASK 2   Children write arm, farm

a. You're going to write the word (pause) **arm**. When you write the word (pause) **arm**, you write these sounds. **Aaa** (pause) **rrr** (pause) **mmm**.

b. Say the sounds you write for (pause) **arm**. Signal for each sound as the children say *aaa* (pause) *rrr* (pause) *mmm*. The children are to pause two seconds between sounds. Repeat until firm.

c. Everybody, write the word (pause) **arm**. Check children's responses.

d. Now you're going to write the word (pause) **farm**. When you write the word (pause) **farm**, you write these sounds. **Fff** (pause) **aaa** (pause) **rrr** (pause) **mmm**.

e. Say the sounds you write for (pause) **farm**. Signal for each sound as the children say *fff* (pause) *aaa* (pause) *rrr* (pause) *mmm*. The children are to pause two seconds between sounds. Repeat until firm.

f. Everybody, write the word (pause) **farm**. Check children's responses.

TASK 3   Children write can

a. You're going to write the word (pause) **can**. This word is tough. I'll say the sounds in (pause) **can** the hard way. Listen. **c** (pause) **aaa** (pause) **nnn**.

b. Your turn. Say the sounds in (pause) **can**. Get ready. Signal for each sound as the children say *c* (pause) *aaa* (pause) *nnn*. The children are to pause two seconds between the sounds. Repeat until firm.

c. Everybody, write the word (pause) **can**. Check children's responses.

TASK 4   Children write did

You're going to write the word **did**. Think about the sounds in (pause) **did** and write the word. Check children's responses.

To correct	**1.** Say the sounds in **did**. (Signal.) *Diiid*. **2.** Say the sounds the hard way. (Signal.) *D* (pause) *iii* (pause) *d*. **3.** Write the word **did**. Check children's responses.

SENTENCE WRITING

TASK 5   Children write a sentence

a. Listen to this sentence. **He was fat**. Say the sentence. Get ready. (Signal.) *He was fat*.

b. Now you're going to say it the slow way. Get ready. Signal for each word as the children say *he* (pause) *was* (pause) *fat*. Repeat until firm.

c. Everybody, write the sentence. Spell each word the right way. As you check children's responses, remind the children: Don't forget to put a period at the end of your sentence.

END OF SPELLING LESSON

Spelling Lesson 87

WORD WRITING

TASK 1   Children write **ant**, **sun**, **can**

a. You're going to write the word **ant**. Think about the sounds in (pause) **ant** and write the word. Check children's responses.

To correct	1. Say the sounds in **ant**. (Signal.) *Aaannnt.*
	2. Say the sounds the hard way. (Signal.) *Aaa* (pause) *nnn* (pause) *t.*
	3. Write the word **ant**. Check children's responses.

b. Repeat *a* for **sun** and **can**.

TASK 2   Children write **arm**, **farm**

a. You're going to write the word (pause) **arm**. When you write the word (pause) **arm**, you write these sounds. **Aaa** (pause) **rrr** (pause) **mmm**.

b. Say the sounds you write for (pause) **arm**. Signal for each sound as the children say *aaa* (pause) *rrr* (pause) *mmm.* The children are to pause two seconds between sounds. Repeat until firm.

c. Everybody, write the word (pause) **arm**. Check children's responses.

d. Now you're going to write the word (pause) **farm**. When you write the word (pause) **farm**, you write these sounds. **Fff** (pause) **aaa** (pause) **rrr** (pause) **mmm**.

e. Say the sounds you write for (pause) **farm**. Signal for each sound as the children say *fff* (pause) *aaa* (pause) *rrr* (pause) *mmm.* The children are to pause two seconds between sounds. Repeat until firm.

f. Everybody, write the word (pause) **farm**. Check children's responses.

TASK 3   Children write **hot**

You're going to write the word **hot**. Think about the sounds in (pause) **hot** and write the word. Check children's responses.

SENTENCE WRITING

TASK 4   Children write a sentence

a. Listen to this sentence. **It is a nut.** Your turn. Say the sentence. Get ready. (Signal.) *It is a nut.*

b. Now you're going to say it the slow way. Get ready. Signal for each word as the children say *it* (pause) *is* (pause) *a* (pause) *nut.* Repeat until firm.

c. Everybody, write the sentence. Spell each word the right way. As you check children's responses, remind the children: **Don't forget to put a period at the end of your sentence.**

END OF SPELLING LESSON

Spelling Lesson 88

WORD WRITING

TASK 1   Children write **arm**

a. You're going to write the word (pause) **arm**. Say the sounds you write for (pause) **arm**. Get ready. Signal for each sound as the children say *aaa* (pause) *rrr* (pause) *mmm.* The children are to pause two seconds between the sounds. Repeat until firm.

b. Everybody, write the word (pause) **arm**. Check children's responses.

TASK 2   Children write **not**, **and**

a. You're going to write the word **not**. Think about the sounds in (pause) **not** and write the word. Check children's responses.

To correct	1. Say the sounds in **not**. (Signal.) *Nnnooot.*
	2. Say the sounds the hard way. (Signal.) *Nnn* (pause) *ooo* (pause) *t.*
	3. Write the word **not**. Check children's responses.

b. Repeat *a* for **and**.

TASK 3   Children write farm

a. You're going to write the word (pause) **farm.** Say the sounds you write for (pause) **farm.** Get ready. Signal for each sound as the children say *fff* (pause) *aaa* (pause) *rrr* (pause) *mmm.* The children are to pause two seconds between the sounds. Repeat until firm.
b. Everybody, write the word (pause) **farm.** Check children's responses.

TASK 4   Children write hid

You're going to write the word **hid.** Think about the sounds in (pause) **hid** and write the word. Check children's responses.

SENTENCE WRITING

TASK 5   Children write a sentence

a. Listen to this sentence. **It is hot.** Your turn. Say the sentence. Get ready. (Signal.) *It is hot.*
b. Now you're going to say it the slow way. Get ready. Signal for each word as the children say *it* (pause) *is* (pause) *hot.* Repeat until firm.
c. Everybody, write the sentence. Spell each word the right way. Check children's responses.

END OF SPELLING LESSON

Spelling Lesson 89

WORD WRITING

TASK 1   Children write farm

a. You're going to write the word (pause) **farm.** Say the sounds you write for (pause) **farm.** Get ready. Signal for each sound as the children say *fff* (pause) *aaa* (pause) *rrr* (pause) *mmm.* The children are to pause two seconds between the sounds. Repeat until firm.
b. Everybody, write the word (pause) **farm.** Check responses.

TASK 2   Children write can

You're going to write the word **can.** Think about the sounds in (pause) **can** and write the word. Check children's responses.

To correct	1. Say the sounds in **can.** (Signal.) *Caaannn.*
	2. Say the sounds the hard way. (Signal.) *C* (pause) *aaa* (pause) *nnn.*
	3. Write the word **can.** Check children's responses.

TASK 3   Children write car

a. You're going to write the word (pause) **car.** When you write the word (pause) **car,** you write these sounds. **C** (pause) **aaa** (pause) **rrr.**
b. Say the sounds you write for (pause) **car.** Signal for each sound as the children say *c* (pause) *aaa* (pause) *rrr.* The children are to pause two seconds between sounds. Repeat until firm.
c. Everybody, write the word (pause) **car.** Check children's responses.

TASK 4   Children write me, sand, hid

a. You're going to write the word **me.** Think about the sounds in (pause) **me** and write the word. Check children's responses.
b. Repeat *a* for **sand** and **hid.**

SENTENCE WRITING

TASK 5   Children write a sentence

a. Listen to this sentence. **He had a fan.** Your turn. Say the sentence. Get ready. (Signal.) *He had a fan.*
b. Now you're going to say it the slow way. Get ready. Signal for each word as the children say *he* (pause) *had* (pause) *a* (pause) *fan.* Repeat until firm.
c. Everybody, write the sentence. Spell each word the right way. Check children's responses.

END OF SPELLING LESSON

Spelling Lesson 90

WORD WRITING

TASK 1   Children write **and, mud, hot**

a. You're going to write the word **and**. Think about the sounds in (pause) **and** and write the word. Check children's responses.

To correct	1. Say the sounds in **and**. (Signal.) *Aaannnd.*
	2. Say the sounds the hard way. (Signal.) *Aaa* (pause) *nnn* (pause) *d.*
	3. Write the word **and**. Check children's responses.

b. Repeat *a* for **mud** and **hot**.

TASK 2   Children write **arm**

a. You're going to write the word (pause) **arm**. Say the sounds you write for (pause) **arm**. Get ready. Signal for each sound as the children say *aaa* (pause) *rrr* (pause) *mmm*. The children are to pause two seconds between the sounds. Repeat until firm.

b. Everybody, write the word (pause) **arm**. Check children's responses.

TASK 3   Children write **car**

a. You're going to write the word (pause) **car**. When you write the word (pause) **car**, you write these sounds. **C** (pause) **aaa** (pause) **rrr.**

b. Say the sounds you write for (pause) **car**. Signal for each sound as the children say *c* (pause) *aaa* (pause) *rrr*. The children are to pause two seconds between sounds. Repeat until firm.

c. Everybody, write the word (pause) **car**. Check children's responses.

TASK 4   Children write **can**

You're going to write the word **can**. Think about the sounds in (pause) **can** and write the word. Check children's responses.

SENTENCE WRITING

TASK 5   Children write a sentence

a. Listen to this sentence. **His dad is sad**. Your turn. Say the sentence. Get ready. (Signal.) *His dad is sad.*

b. Now you're going to say it the slow way. Get ready. Signal for each word as the children say *his* (pause) *dad* (pause) *is* (pause) *sad*. Repeat until firm.

c. Everybody, write the sentence. Spell each word the right way. Check children's responses.

END OF SPELLING LESSON

Spelling Lesson 91

WORD WRITING

TASK 1   Children write **car, far, tar**

a. You're going to write the word (pause) **car**. When you write the word (pause) **car**, you write these sounds. **C** (pause) **aaa** (pause) **rrr.**

b. Say the sounds you write for (pause) **car**. Signal for each sound as the children say *c* (pause) *aaa* (pause) *rrr*. The children are to pause two seconds between sounds. Repeat until firm.

c. Everybody, write the word (pause) **car**. Check responses.

d. Now you're going to write the word (pause) **far**. When you write the word (pause) **far**, you write these sounds. **Fff** (pause) **aaa** (pause) **rrr.**

e. Say the sounds you write for (pause) **far**. Signal for each sound as the children say *fff* (pause) *aaa* (pause) *rrr*. The children are to pause two seconds between sounds. Repeat until firm.

f. Everybody, write the word (pause) **far**. Check responses.

g. Next you're going to write the word (pause) **tar**. When you write the word (pause) **tar**, you write these sounds. **T** (pause) **aaa** (pause) **rrr.**

h. Say the sounds you write for (pause) **tar**. Signal for each sound as the children say *t* (pause) *aaa* (pause) *rrr*. The children are to pause two seconds between sounds. Repeat until firm.

i. Everybody, write the word (pause) **tar**. Check responses.

TASK 2   Children write arm, farm

a. You're going to write the word **arm**. Think about the sounds in (pause) **arm** and write the word. Check children's responses.

| To correct | 1. Say the sounds the hard way. (Signal.) *Aaa* (pause) *rrr* (pause) *mmm*. |
| | 2. Write the word **arm**. Check children's responses. |

b. Repeat *a* for **farm**.

SENTENCE WRITING

TASK 3   Children write a sentence

a. Listen to this sentence. **His dad has sand**. Your turn. Say that sentence. Get ready. (Signal.) *His dad has sand*.

b. Now you're going to say it the slow way. Get ready. Signal for each word as the children say *his* (pause) *dad* (pause) *has* (pause) *sand*. Repeat until firm.

c. Everybody, write the sentence. Spell each word the right way. Check children's responses.

END OF SPELLING LESSON

Spelling Lesson 92

WORD WRITING

TASK 1   Children write are

a. You're going to write the word (pause) **are**. When you write the word (pause) **are**, you write these sounds. **Aaa** (pause) **rrr** (pause) **ēēē**.

b. Say the sounds you write for (pause) **are**. Signal for each sound as the children say *aaa* (pause) *rrr* (pause) *ēēē*. The children are to pause two seconds between sounds. Repeat until firm.

c. Everybody, write the word (pause) **are**. Check children's responses.

TASK 2   Children write far, car

a. You're going to write the word (pause) **far**. Say the sounds you write for (pause) **far**. Get ready. Signal for each sound as the children say *fff* (pause) *aaa* (pause) *rrr*. The children are to pause two seconds between the sounds. Repeat until firm.

b. Everybody, write the word (pause) **far**. Check children's responses.

c. Now you're going to write the word (pause) **car**. Say the sounds you write for (pause) **car**. Signal for each sound as the children say *c* (pause) *aaa* (pause) *rrr*. The children are to pause two seconds between sounds. Repeat until firm.

d. Everybody, write the word (pause) **car**. Check children's responses.

TASK 3   Children write not, land

a. You're going to write the word **not**. Think about the sounds in (pause) **not** and write the word. Check children's responses.

To correct	1. Say the sounds in **not**. (Signal.) *Nnnooot*.
	2. Say the sounds the hard way. (Signal.) *Nnn* (pause) *ooo* (pause) *t*.
	3. Write the word **not**. Check children's responses.

b. Repeat *a* for **land**.

SENTENCE WRITING

TASK 4   Children write a sentence

a. Listen to this sentence. **He has a dad**. Your turn. Say that sentence. Get ready. (Signal.) *He has a dad*.

b. Now you're going to say it the slow way. Get ready. Signal for each word as the children say *he* (pause) *has* (pause) *a* (pause) *dad*. Repeat until firm.

c. Everybody, write the sentence. Spell each word the right way. Check children's responses.

END OF SPELLING LESSON

Spelling Lesson 93

WORD WRITING

TASK 1 Children write **car**

a. You're going to write the word (pause) **car**. Say the sounds you write for (pause) **car**. Get ready. Signal for each sound as the children say *c* (pause) *aaa* (pause) *rrr.* The children are to pause two seconds between the sounds. Repeat until firm.

b. Everybody, write the word (pause) **car**. Check children's responses.

TASK 2 Children write **tan**

a. You're going to write the word **was**. Think about the sounds in (pause) **was** and write the word. Check children's responses.

To correct	1. Say the sounds in **tan**. (Signal.) *Taaannn.* 2. Say the sounds the hard way. (Signal.) *T* (pause) *aaa* (pause) *nnn.* 3. Write the word **tan**. Check children's responses.

TASK 3 Children write **are**

a. You're going to write the word (pause) **are**. When you write the word (pause) **are**, you write these sounds. **Aaa** (pause) **rrr** (pause) **ēēē**.

b. Say the sounds you write for (pause) **are**. Signal for each sound as the children say *aaa* (pause) *rrr* (pause) *ēēē.* The children are to pause two seconds between sounds. Repeat until firm.

c. Write the word (pause) **are**. Check children's responses.

TASK 4 Children write **was, can**

a. You're going to write the word **was**. Think about the sounds in (pause) **was** and write the word. Check children's responses.

To correct	1. Say the sounds the hard way. (Signal.) *Www* (pause) *aaa* (pause) *sss.* 2. Write the word **was**. Check children's responses.

b. Repeat a for **can.**

TASK 5 Children write **far**

a. You're going to write the word (pause) **far**. Say the sounds you write for (pause) **far**. Get ready. Signal for each sound as the children say *fff* (pause) *aaa* (pause) *rrr.* The children are to pause two seconds between the sounds. Repeat until firm.

b. Everybody, write the word (pause) **far**. Check children's responses.

SENTENCE WRITING

TASK 6 Children write a sentence

a. Listen to this sentence. **A farm is fun**. Your turn. Say that sentence. Get ready. (Signal.) *A farm is fun.*

b. Now you're going to say it the slow way. Get ready. Signal for each word as the children say *a* (pause) *farm* (pause) *is* (pause) *fun.* Repeat until firm.

c. Everybody, write the sentence. Spell each word the right way. Check children's responses.

END OF SPELLING LESSON

Spelling Lesson 94

WORD WRITING

TASK 1 Children write **are**

a. You're going to write the word (pause) **are**. Say the sounds you write for (pause) **are**. Get ready. Signal for each sound as the children say *aaa* (pause) *rrr* (pause) *ēēē.* The children are to pause two seconds between the sounds. Repeat until firm.

b. Everybody, write the word (pause) **are**. Check children's responses.

TASK 2   Children write **hard**

a. You're going to write the word (pause) **hard**. When you write the word (pause) **hard**, you write these sounds. **H** (pause) **aaa** (pause) **rrr** (pause) **d**.

b. Say the sounds you write for (pause) **hard**. Signal for each sound as the children say *h* (pause) *aaa* (pause) *rrr* (pause) *d.* The children are to pause two seconds between sounds. Repeat until firm.

c. Everybody, write the word (pause) **hard**. Check children's responses.

TASK 3   Children write **car**

a. You're going to write the word (pause) **car**. Say the sounds you write for (pause) **car**. Get ready. Signal for each sound as the children say *c* (pause) *aaa* (pause) *rrr.* The children are to pause two seconds between the sounds. Repeat until firm.

b. Everybody, write the word (pause) **car**. Check children's responses.

TASK 4   Children write **card**

a. You're going to write the word (pause) **card**. When you write the word (pause) **card**, you write these sounds. **C** (pause) **aaa** (pause) **rrr** (pause) **d**.

b. Say the sounds you write for (pause) **card**. Signal for each sound as the children say *c* (pause) *aaa* (pause) *rrr* (pause) *d.* The children are to pause two seconds between the sounds. Repeat until firm.

c. Everybody, write the word (pause) **card**. Check children's responses.

TASK 5   Children write **nod**

You're going to write the word **nod**. Think about the sounds in (pause) **nod** and write the word. Check children's responses.

To correct	1. Say the sounds in **nod**. (Signal.) *Nnnoood.* 2. Say the sounds the hard way. (Signal.) *Nnn* (pause) *ooo* (pause) *d.* 3. Write the word **nod**. Check children's responses.

SENTENCE WRITING

TASK 6   Children write a sentence

a. Listen to this sentence. **I am not sad**. Your turn. Say that sentence. Get ready. (Signal.) *I am not sad.*

b. Now you're going to say it the slow way. Get ready. Signal for each word as the children say *I* (pause) *am* (pause) *not* (pause) *sad.* Repeat until firm.

c. Everybody, write the sentence. Spell each word the right way. Check children's responses.

END OF SPELLING LESSON

Spelling Lesson 95

SOUND WRITING

TASK 1   Children write **b**

a. You're going to write a sound.

b. Here's the sound you're going to write. Listen. **b**. What sound? (Signal.) *b.*

c. Write **b**. Check children's responses.

WORD WRITING

TASK 2   Children write **we**, **hid**

a. You're going to write the word **we**. Think about the sounds in (pause) **we** and write the word. Check children's responses.

To correct	1. Say the sounds in **we**. (Signal.) *Wwwēēē.* 2. Say the sounds the hard way. (Signal.) *Www* (pause) *ēēē.* 3. Write the word **we**. Check children's responses.

b. Repeat *a* for **hid**.

TASK 3   Children write **are**

a. You're going to write the word (pause) **are**. Say the sounds you write for (pause) **are**. Get ready. Signal for each sound as the children say *aaa* (pause) *rrr* (pause) *ēēē*. The children are to pause two seconds between the sounds. Repeat until firm.

b. Everybody, write the word (pause) **are**. Check children's responses.

TASK 4   Children write **was**, **has**, **can**

a. You're going to write the word **was**. Think about the sounds in (pause) **was** and write the word. Check children's responses.

To correct	1. Say the sounds the hard way. (Signal.) *Www* (pause) *aaa* (pause) *sss*.
	2. Write the word **was**. Check children's responses.

b. Repeat *a* for **has** and **can**.

SENTENCE WRITING

TASK 5   Children write a sentence

a. Listen to this sentence. **His dad was mad.** Your turn. Say that sentence. Get ready. (Signal.) *His dad was mad.*

b. Now you're going to say it the slow way. Get ready. Signal for each word as the children say *his* (pause) *dad* (pause) *was* (pause) *mad*. Repeat until firm.

c. Everybody, write the sentence. Spell each word the right way. Check children's responses.

END OF SPELLING LESSON

Spelling Lesson 96

SOUND WRITING

TASK 1   Children write **b**

a. You're going to write a sound.

b. Here's the sound you're going to write. Listen. **b.** What sound? (Signal.) *b.*

c. Write **b**. Check children's responses.

WORD WRITING

TASK 2   Children write **are**, **sit**

a. You're going to write the word **are**. Think about the sounds in (pause) **are** and write the word. Check children's responses.

To correct	1. Say the sounds the hard way. (Signal.) *Aaa* (pause) *rrr* (pause) *ēēē*.
	2. Write the word **are**. Check children's responses.

b. Repeat *a* for **sit**.

TASK 3   Children write **bit**

a. You're going to write the word (pause) **bit**. This word is tough. I'll say the sounds in (pause) **bit** the hard way. Listen. **B** (pause) **iii** (pause) **t**.

b. Your turn. Say the sounds in (pause) **bit**. Get ready. Signal for each sound as the children say *b* (pause) *iii* (pause) *t*. The children are to pause two seconds between sounds. Repeat until firm.

c. Everybody, write the word (pause) **bit**. Check children's responses.

TASK 4   Children write **land**

You're going to write the word **land**. Think about the sounds in (pause) **land** and write the word. Check children's responses.

TASK 5   Children write card

a. You're going to write the word (pause) **card**. Say the sounds you write for (pause) **card**. Get ready. Signal for each sound as the children say c (pause) aaa (pause) rrr (pause) d. The children are to pause two seconds between the sounds. Repeat until firm.

b. Everybody, write the word (pause) **card**. Check children's responses.

TASK 6   Children write cat

a. You're going to write the word **cat**. Listen. **Cat**. Saying the sounds in (pause) **cat** the hard way. Get ready. Signal for each sound as the children say c (pause) aaa (pause) t. The children are to pause two seconds between the sounds. Repeat until firm.

b. Everybody, write the word (pause) **cat**. Check children's responses.

SENTENCE WRITING

TASK 7   Children write a sentence

a. Listen to this sentence. **I am not fat**. Your turn. Say that sentence. Get ready. (Signal.) I am not fat.

b. Now you're going to say it the slow way. Get ready. Signal for each word as the children say I (pause) am (pause) not (pause) fat. Repeat until firm.

c. Everybody, write the sentence. Spell each word the right way. Check children's responses.

END OF SPELLING LESSON

Spelling Lesson 97

WORD WRITING

TASK 1   Children write card, farm, is

a. You're going to write the word **card**. Think about the sounds in (pause) **card** and write the word. Check children's responses.

To correct	1. Say the sounds the hard way. (Signal.) C (pause) aaa (pause) rrr (pause) d.
	2. Write the word **card**. Check children's responses.

b. Repeat a for **farm** and **is**.

TASK 2   Children write bit

a. You're going to write the word (pause) **bit**. This word is tough. I'll say the sounds in (pause) **bit** the hard way. Listen. **B** (pause) **iii** (pause) **t**.

b. Your turn. Say the sounds in (pause) **bit**. Get ready. Signal for each sound as the children say b (pause) iii (pause) t. The children are to pause two seconds between the sounds. Repeat until firm.

c. Everybody, write the word (pause) **bit**. Check children's responses.

TASK 3   Children write not

You're going to write the word **not**. Think about the sounds in (pause) **not** and write the word.

To correct	1. Say the sounds in **not**. (Signal.) Nnnooot.
	2. Say the sounds the hard way. (Signal.) Nnn (pause) ooo (pause) t.
	3. Write the word **not**. Check children's responses.

SENTENCE WRITING

TASK 4   Children write a sentence

a. Listen to this sentence. **He did run far**. Your turn. Say that sentence. Get ready. (Signal.) *He did run far.*
b. Now you're going to say it the slow way. Get ready. Signal for each word as the children say *he* (pause) *did* (pause) *run* (pause) *far.* Repeat until firm.
c. Everybody, write the sentence. Spell each word the right way. Check children's responses.

END OF SPELLING LESSON

Spelling Lesson 98

WORD WRITING

TASK 1   Children write **bad**

a. You're going to write the word (pause) **bad**. This word is tough. I'll say the sounds in (pause) **bad** the hard way. Listen. **B** (pause) **aaa** (pause) **d**.
b. Your turn. Say the sounds in (pause) **bad**. Get ready. Signal for each sound as the children say *b* (pause) *aaa* (pause) *d*. The children are to pause two seconds between the sounds. Repeat until firm.
c. Everybody, write the word (pause) **bad**. Check children's responses.

TASK 2   Children write **are**, **his**, **card**

a. You're going to write the word **are**. Think about the sounds in (pause) **are** and write the word. Check children's responses.

To correct	1. Say the sounds the hard way. (Signal.) *Aaa* (pause) *rrr* (pause) *ēēē.*
	2. Write the word **are**. Check children's responses.

b. Repeat *a* for **his** and **card**.

TASK 3   Children write **cart**

a. You're going to write the word (pause) **cart**. Say the sounds you write for (pause) **cart**. Get ready. Signal for each sound as the children say *c* (pause) *aaa* (pause) *rrr* (pause) *t*. The children are to pause two seconds between the sounds. Repeat until firm.
b. Everybody, write the word (pause) **cart**. Check children's responses.

TASK 4   Children write **cat**

a. You're going to write the word **cat**. Listen. **Cat**. Saying the sounds in (pause) **cat** the hard way. Get ready. Signal for each sound as the children say *c* (pause) *aaa* (pause) *t*. The children are to pause two seconds between the sounds. Repeat until firm.
b. Everybody, write the word (pause) **cat**. Check children's responses.

SENTENCE WRITING

TASK 5   Children write a sentence

a. Listen to this sentence. **We are not sad**. Your turn. Say that sentence. Get ready. (Signal.) *We are not sad.*
b. Now you're going to say it the slow way. Get ready. Signal for each word as the children say *we* (pause) *are* (pause) *not* (pause) *sad.* Repeat until firm.
c. Everybody, write the sentence. Spell each word the right way. Check children's responses.

END OF SPELLING LESSON

Spelling Lesson 99

WORD WRITING

TASK 1 Children write **was, can**

a. You're going to write the word **was**. Think about the sounds in (pause) **was** and write the word. Check children's responses.

To correct	1. Say the sounds the hard way. (Signal.) *Www* (pause) *aaa* (pause) *sss*.
	2. Write the word **was**. Check children's responses.

b. You're going to write the word **can**. Think about the sounds in (pause) **can** and write the word. Check children's responses.

To correct	1. Say the sounds in **can**. (Signal.) *Caaannn*.
	2. Say the sounds the hard way. (Signal.) *C* (pause) *aaa* (pause) *nnn*.
	3. Write the word **can**. Check children's responses.

TASK 2 Children write **cat**

a. You're going to write the word **cat**. Listen. **Cat**. Saying the sounds in (pause) **cat** the hard way. Get ready. Signal for each sound as the children say *c* (pause) *aaa* (pause) *t*. The children are to pause two seconds between the sounds. Repeat until firm.

b. Everybody, write the word (pause) **cat**. Check children's responses.

TASK 3 Children write **see**

a. You're going to write the word (pause) **see**. When you write the word (pause) **see**, you write these sounds. **Sss** (pause) $\bar{e}\bar{e}\bar{e}$ (pause) $\bar{e}\bar{e}\bar{e}$.

b. Say the sounds you write for (pause) **see**. Signal for each sound as the children say *sss* (pause) $\bar{e}\bar{e}\bar{e}$ (pause) $\bar{e}\bar{e}\bar{e}$. The children are to pause two seconds between the sounds. Repeat until firm.

c. Write the word (pause) **see**. Check children's responses.

TASK 4 Children write **farm**

You're going to write the word **farm**. Think about the sounds in (pause) **farm** and write the word. Check children's responses.

TASK 5 Children write **but**

a. You're going to write the word (pause) **but**. This word is tough. I'll say the sounds in (pause) **but** the hard way. Listen. **B** (pause) **uuu** (pause) **t**.

b. Your turn. Say the sounds in (pause) **but**. Get ready. Signal for each sound as the children say *b* (pause) *uuu* (pause) *t*. The children are to pause two seconds between sounds. Repeat until firm.

c. Everybody, write the word (pause) **but**. Check children's responses.

SENTENCE WRITING

TASK 6 Children write a sentence

a. Listen to this sentence. **I am in mud**. Your turn. Say that sentence. Get ready. (Signal.) *I am in mud.*

b. Now you're going to say it the slow way. Get ready. Signal for each word as the children say *I* (pause) *am* (pause) *in* (pause) *mud*. Repeat until firm.

c. Everybody, write the sentence. Spell each word the right way. Check children's responses.

END OF SPELLING LESSON

Spelling Lesson 100

WORD WRITING

TASK 1   Children write **see**

a. You're going to write the word (pause) **see**. When you write the word (pause) **see**, you write these sounds. **Sss** (pause) ē̄ēē (pause) ē̄ēē.

b. Say the sounds you write for (pause) **see**. Signal for each sound as the children say *sss* (pause) *ē̄ēē* (pause) *ē̄ēē*. The children are to pause two seconds between sounds. Repeat until firm.

c. Write the word (pause) **see**. Check children's responses.

TASK 2   Children write **but**

a. You're going to write the word (pause) **but**. This word is tough. I'll say the sounds in (pause) **but** the hard way. Listen. **B** (pause) **uuu** (pause) **t**.

b. Your turn. Say the sounds in (pause) **but**. Get ready. Signal for each sound as the children say *b* (pause) *uuu* (pause) *t*. The children are to pause two seconds between the sounds. Repeat until firm.

c. Everybody, write the word (pause) **but**. Check children's responses.

TASK 3   Children write **his**

You're going to write the word **his**. Think about the sounds in (pause) **his** and write the word. Check children's responses.

To correct	1. Say the sounds the hard way. (Signal.) *H* (pause) *iii* (pause) *sss*.
	2. Write the word **his**. Check children's responses.

TASK 4   Children write **bit**

a. You're going to write the word **bit**. Listen. **Bit**. Saying the sounds in (pause) **bit** the hard way. Get ready. Signal for each sound as the children say *b* (pause) *iii* (pause) *t*. The children are to pause two seconds between the sounds. Repeat until firm.

b. Everybody, write the word (pause) **bit**. Check children's responses.

SENTENCE WRITING

TASK 5   Children write a sentence

a. Listen to this sentence. **We are in sand**. Your turn. Say the sentence. Get ready. (Signal.) *We are in sand.*

b. Now you're going to say it the slow way. Get ready. Signal for each word as the children say *we* (pause) *are* (pause) *in* (pause) *sand*. Repeat until firm.

c. Everybody, write the sentence. Spell each word the right way. Check children's responses.

END OF SPELLING LESSON

Spelling Lesson 101

WORD WRITING

TASK 1   Children write **bad**

a. You're going to write the word (pause) **bad**. Say the sounds you write for (pause) **bad**. Get ready. Signal for each sound as the children say *b* (pause) *aaa* (pause) *d*. The children are to pause two seconds between the sounds. Repeat until firm.

b. Everybody, write the word (pause) **bad**. Check children's responses.

TASK 2   Children write **see**

a. You're going to write the word (pause) **see**. When you write the word (pause) **see**, you write these sounds. **Sss** (pause) ē̄ēē (pause) ē̄ēē.

b. Say the sounds you write for (pause) **see**. Signal for each sound as the children say *sss* (pause) *ē̄ēē* (pause) *ē̄ēē*. The children are to pause two seconds between sounds. Repeat until firm.

c. Write the word (pause) **see**. Check children's responses.

TASK 3   Children write **but**

a. You're going to write the word (pause) **but**. Say the sounds you write for (pause) **but**. Get ready. Signal for each sound as the children say *b* (pause) *uuu* (pause) *t*. The children are to pause two seconds between the sounds. Repeat until firm.

b. Everybody, write the word (pause) **but**. Check children's responses.

TASK 4   Children write **and**

You're going to write the word **and**. Think about the sounds in (pause) **and** and write the word. Check children's responses.

TASK 5   Children write **bit**

a. You're going to write the word (pause) **bit**. Say the sounds you write for (pause) **bit**. Get ready. Signal for each sound as the children say *b* (pause) *iii* (pause) *t*. The children are to pause two seconds between the sounds. Repeat until firm.

b. Everybody, write the word (pause) **bit**. Check children's responses.

SENTENCE WRITING

TASK 6   Children write a sentence

a. Listen to this sentence. **We are on land**. Your turn. Say that sentence. Get ready. (Signal.) *We are on land*.

b. Now you're going to say it the slow way. Get ready. Signal for each word as the children say *we* (pause) *are* (pause) *on* (pause) *land*. Repeat until firm.

c. Everybody, write the sentence. Spell each word the right way. Check children's responses.

END OF SPELLING LESSON

Spelling Lesson 102

SOUND WRITING

TASK 1   Children write **th**

a. You're going to write a sound.

b. Here's the sound you're going to write. Listen. **thththth**. What sound? (Signal.) *thththth*

c. Write **thththth**. Check children's responses.

WORD WRITING

TASK 2   Children write **bit**

You're going to write the word **bit**. Think about the sounds in (pause) **bit** and write the word. Check children's responses.

To correct	1. Say the sounds in **bit**. (Signal.) *Biiit*.
	2. Say the sounds the hard way. (Signal.) *B* (pause) *iii* (pause) *t*.
	3. Write the word **bit**. Check children's responses.

TASK 3   Children write **see**

a. You're going to write the word (pause) **see**. Say the sounds you write for (pause) **see**. Get ready. Signal for each sound as the children say *sss* (pause) *ēēē* (pause) *ēēē*. The children are to pause two seconds between the sounds. Repeat until firm.

b. Everybody, write the word (pause) **see**. Check children's responses.

TASK 4   Children write **can**, **but**, **card**

a. You're going to write the word **can**. Think about the sounds in (pause) **can** and write the word. Check children's responses.

b. Repeat *a* for **but**.

c. You're going to write the word **card**. Think about the sounds in (pause) **card** and write the word.

| To correct | 1. Say the sounds the hard way. (Signal.) *C* (pause) *aaa* (pause) *rrr* (pause) *d*. |
| | 2. Write the word **card**. Check children's responses. |

SENTENCE WRITING

TASK 5   Children write a sentence

a. Listen to this sentence. **We had a car**. Your turn. Say that sentence. Get ready. (Signal.) *We had a car.*

b. Now you're going to say it the slow way. Get ready. Signal for each word as the children say *we* (pause) *had* (pause) *a* (pause) *car*. Repeat until firm.

c. Everybody, write the sentence. Spell each word the right way. Check children's responses.

END OF SPELLING LESSON

Spelling Lesson 103

SOUND WRITING

TASK 1   Children write **th**

a. You're going to write a sound.

b. Here's the sound you're going to write. Listen. **ththth**. What sound? (Signal.) *ththth.*

c. Write **ththth**. Check children's responses.

WORD WRITING

TASK 2   Children write **are, bad**

a. You're going to write the word **are**. Think about the sounds in (pause) **are** and write the word. Check children's responses.

To correct	1. Say the sounds the hard way. (Signal.) *Aaa* (pause) *rrr* (pause) *ēēē.*
	2. Write the word **are**. Check children's responses.

b. Repeat *a* for **bad**.

TASK 3   Children write **thē**

a. You're going to write the word (pause) **thē**. This word is tough. I'll say the sounds in (pause) **thē** the hard way. Listen. **Ththth** (pause) **ēēē**.

b. Your turn. Say the sounds in (pause) **thē**. Get ready. Signal for each sound as the children say *ththth* (pause) *ēēē*. The children are to pause two seconds between the sounds. Repeat until firm.

c. Everybody, write the word (pause) **thē**. Check children's responses.

TASK 4   Children write **this, that**

a. You're going to write the word **this**. Listen. **This**. Saying the sounds in (pause) **this** the hard way. Get ready. Signal for each sound as the children say *ththth* (pause) *iii* (pause) *sss*. The children are to pause two seconds between the sounds. Repeat until firm.

b. Everybody, write the word (pause) **this**. Check children's responses.

c. Repeat *a* and *b* for **that**.

SENTENCE WRITING

TASK 5   Children write a sentence

a. Listen to this sentence. **He has a farm**. Your turn. Say that sentence. Get ready. (Signal.) *He has a farm.*

b. Now you're going to say it the slow way. Get ready. Signal for each word as the children say *he* (pause) *has* (pause) *a* (pause) *farm*. Repeat until firm.

c. Everybody, write the sentence. Spell each word the right way. Check children's responses.

END OF SPELLING LESSON

Spelling Lesson 104

WORD WRITING

TASK 1 Children write **that**

a. You're going to write the word **that**. Listen. **That**. Saying the sounds in (pause) **that** the hard way. Get ready. Signal for each sound as the children say *ththth* (pause) *aaa* (pause) *t*. The children are to pause two seconds between the sounds. Repeat until firm.

b. Everybody, write the word (pause) **that**. Check children's responses.

TASK 2 Children write **see**

a. You're going to write the word (pause) **see**. Say the sounds you write for (pause) **see**. Get ready. Signal for each sound as the children say *sss* (pause) *ēēē* (pause) *ēēē*. The children are to pause two seconds between the sounds. Repeat until firm.

b. Everybody, write the word (pause) **see**. Check children's responses.

TASK 3 Children write **the̅**

a. You're going to write the word **the̅**. Listen. **The̅**. Saying the sounds in (pause) **the̅** the hard way. Get ready. Signal for each sound as the children say *ththth* (pause) *ēēē*. The children are to pause two seconds between the sounds. Repeat until firm.

b. Everybody, write the word (pause) **the̅**. Check children's responses.

TASK 4 Children write **are**

You're going to write the word **are**. Think about the sounds in (pause) **are** and write the word. Check children's responses.

To correct	1. Say the sounds the hard way. (Signal.) *Aaa* (pause) *rrr* (pause) *ēēē*.
	2. Write the word **are**. Check children's responses.

TASK 5 Children write **this**

a. You're going to write the word **this**. Listen. **This**. Saying the sounds in (pause) **this** the hard way. Get ready. Signal for each sound as the children say *ththth* (pause) *iii* (pause) *sss*. The children are to pause two seconds between the sounds. Repeat until firm.

b. Everybody, write the word (pause) **this**. Check children's responses.

SENTENCE WRITING

TASK 6 Children write a sentence

a. Listen to this sentence. **He did not run**. Your turn. Say that sentence. Get ready. (Signal.) *He did not run*.

b. Now you're going to say it the slow way. Get ready. Signal for each word as the children say *he* (pause) *did* (pause) *not* (pause) *run*. Repeat until firm.

c. Everybody, write the sentence. Spell each word the right way. Check children's responses.

END OF SPELLING LESSON

Spelling Lesson 105

WORD WRITING

TASK 1 Children write **will**

a. You're going to write the word (pause) **will**. When you write the word (pause) **will**, you write these sounds. **Www** (pause) *iii* (pause) *lll* (pause) *lll*.

b. Say the sounds you write for (pause) **will**. Signal for each sound as the children say *www* (pause) *iii* (pause) *lll* (pause) *lll*. The children are to pause two seconds between sounds. Repeat until firm.

c. Everybody, write the word (pause) **will**. Check children's responses.

TASK 2 Children write **arm**

You're going to write the word **arm**. Think about the sounds in (pause) **arm** and write the word. Check children's responses.

| To correct | 1. Say the sounds the hard way. (Signal.) *Aaa* (pause) *rrr* (pause) *mmm*. |
| | 2. Write the word **arm**. Check children's responses. |

TASK 3 Children write **barn**

a. You're going to write the word (pause) **barn**. When you write the word (pause) **barn**, you write these sounds. **B** (pause) **aaa** (pause) **rrr** (pause) **nnn**.

b. Say the sounds you write for (pause) **barn**. Signal for each sound as the children say *b* (pause) *aaa* (pause) *rrr* (pause) *nnn*. The children are to pause two seconds between sounds. Repeat until firm.

c. Everybody, write the word (pause) **barn**. Check children's responses.

TASK 4 Children write **that**

a. You're going to write the word **that**. Listen. **That**. Saying the sounds in (pause) **that** the hard way. Get ready. Signal for each sound as the children say *thththth* (pause) *aaa* (pause) *t*. The children are to pause two seconds between the sounds. Repeat until firm.

b. Everybody, write the word (pause) **that**. Check children's responses.

TASK 5 Children write **can**

You're going to write the word **can**. Think about the sounds in (pause) **can** and write the word. Check children's responses.

SENTENCE WRITING

TASK 6 Children write a sentence

a. Listen to this sentence. **We are in the sand**. Your turn. Say that sentence. Get ready. (Signal.) *We are in the sand.*

b. Now you're going to say it the slow way. Get ready. Signal for each word as the children say *we* (pause) *are* (pause) *in* (pause) *the* (pause) *sand*. Repeat until firm.

c. Everybody, write the sentence. Spell each word the right way. Check children's responses.

END OF SPELLING LESSON

Spelling Lesson 106

WORD WRITING

TASK 1 Children write **see**

a. You're going to write the word (pause) **see**. Say the sounds you write for (pause) **see**. Get ready. Signal for each sound as the children say *sss* (pause) *ēēē* (pause) *ēēē*. The children are to pause two seconds between the sounds. Repeat until firm.

b. Everybody, write the word (pause) **see**. Check children's responses.

TASK 2 Children write **this**

a. You're going to write the word **this**. Think about the sounds in (pause) **this** and write the word. Check children's responses.

To correct	1. Say the sounds in **this**. (Signal.) *Thththiiisss*.
	2. Say the sounds the hard way. (Signal.) *Thththth* (pause) *iii* (pause) *sss*.
	3. Write the word **this**. Check children's responses.

TASK 3   Children write will

a. You're going to write the word   (pause) **will**. When you write the word   (pause) **will**, you write these sounds. **Www** (pause) **iii** (pause) **lll** (pause) **lll**.

b. Say the sounds you write for   (pause) **will**. Signal for each sound as the children say *www* (pause) *iii* (pause) *lll* (pause) *lll*. The children are to pause two seconds between the sounds. Repeat until firm.

c. Everybody, write the word   (pause) **will**. Check responses.

TASK 4   Children write barn

a. You're going to write the word   (pause) **barn**. Say the sounds you write for   (pause) **barn**. Get ready.   Signal for each sound as the children say *b* (pause) *aaa* (pause) *rrr* (pause) *nnn*. The children are to pause two seconds between the sounds. Repeat until firm.

b. Everybody, write the word   (pause) **barn**. Check responses.

TASK 5   Children write thē, cat

a. You're going to write the word **thē**. Think about the sounds in   (pause) **thē** and write the word. Check children's responses.

To correct	1. Say the sounds in **thē**. (Signal.) *Thththēēē.* 2. Say the sounds the hard way. (Signal.) *Thththth* (pause) *ēēē.* 3. Write the word **thē**. Check children's responses.

b. Repeat *a* for **cat**.

SENTENCE WRITING

TASK 6   Children write a sentence

a. Listen to this sentence. **The ant was bad**. Your turn. Say that sentence. Get ready. (Signal.) *The ant was bad.*

b. Now you're going to say it the slow way. Get ready. Signal for each word as the children say *the* (pause) *ant* (pause) *was* (pause) *bad*. Repeat until firm.

c. Everybody, write the sentence. Spell each word the right way. Check children's responses.

Spelling Lesson 107

SOUND WRITING

TASK 1   Children write p

a. You're going to write a sound.

b. Here's the sound you're going to write. Listen. **p**. What sound? (Signal.) *p.*

c. Write **p**. Check children's responses.

WORD WRITING

TASK 2   Children write but, that, cat

a. You're going to write the word **but**. Think about the sounds in   (pause) **but** and write the word. Check children's responses.

To correct	1. Say the sounds in **but**. (Signal.) *Buuut.* 2. Say the sounds the hard way. (Signal.) *B* (pause) *uuu* (pause) *t.* 3. Write the word **but**. Check children's responses.

b. Repeat *a* for **that** and **cat**.

TASK 3   Children write will

a. You're going to write the word   (pause) **will**. Say the sounds you write for   (pause) **will**. Get ready. Signal for each sound as the children say *www* (pause) *iii* (pause) *lll* (pause) *lll*. The children are to pause two seconds between the sounds. Repeat until firm.

b. Everybody, write the word   (pause) **will**. Check children's responses.

TASK 4   Children write see

You're going to write the word **see**. Think about the sounds in   (pause) **see** and write the word. Check children's responses.

To correct	1. Say the sounds the hard way. (Signal.) *Sss* (pause) *ēēē* (pause) *ēēē.* 2. Write the word **see**. Check children's responses.

SENTENCE WRITING

TASK 5   Children write a sentence

a. Listen to this sentence. **This car is tan**. Your turn. Say that sentence. Get ready. (Signal.) *This car is tan.*

b. Now you're going to say it the slow way. Get ready. Signal for each word as the children say *this* (pause) *car* (pause) *is* (pause) *tan*. Repeat until firm.

c. Everybody, write the sentence. Spell each word the right way. Check children's responses.

END OF SPELLING LESSON

Spelling Lesson 108

SOUND WRITING

TASK 1   Children write p

a. You're going to write a sound.
b. Here's the sound you're going to write. Listen. **p**.
What sound? (Signal.) *p.*

c. Write **p**. Check children's responses.

WORD WRITING

TASK 2   Children write bill

a. You're going to write the word (pause) **bill**. When you write the word (pause) **bill**, you write these sounds. **B** (pause) **iii** (pause) **lll** (pause) **lll**.

b. Say the sounds you write for (pause) **bill**. Signal for each sound as the children say *b* (pause) *iii* (pause) *lll* (pause) *lll*. The children are to pause two seconds between the sounds. Repeat until firm.

c. Everybody, write the word (pause) **bill**. Check children's responses.

TASK 3   Children write will

a. You're going to write the word (pause) **will**. Say the sounds you write for (pause) **will**. Get ready. Signal for each sound as the children say *www* (pause) *iii* (pause) *lll* (pause) *lll*. The children are to pause two seconds between the sounds. Repeat until firm.

b. Everybody, write the word (pause) **will**. Check children's responses.

TASK 4   Children write are, the, but

a. You're going to write the word **are**. Think about the sounds in (pause) **are** and write the word. Check children's responses.

To correct	1. Say the sounds the hard way. (Signal.) *Aaa* (pause) *rrr* (pause) *ēēē.*
	2. Write the word **are**. Check children's responses.

b. You're going to write the word **thē**. Think about the sounds in (pause) **thē** and write the word. Check children's responses.

To correct	1. Say the sounds in **thē**. (Signal.) *Thththēēē.*
	2. Say the sounds the hard way. (Signal.) *Thththth* (pause) *ēēē.*
	3. Write the word **thē**. Check children's responses.

c. Repeat *b* for **but**.

SENTENCE WRITING

TASK 5   Children write a sentence

a. Listen to this sentence. **It is a fat ant**. Your turn. Say that sentence. Get ready. (Signal.) *It is a fat ant.*

b. Now you're going to say it the slow way. Get ready. Signal for each word as the children say *it* (pause) *is* (pause) *a* (pause) *fat* (pause) *ant*. Repeat until firm.

c. Everybody, write the sentence. Spell each word the right way. Check children's responses.

END OF SPELLING LESSON

Spelling Lesson 109

WORD WRITING

TASK 1 Children write see

You're going to write the word **see**. Think about the sounds in (pause) **see** and write the word. Check children's responses.

To correct	1. Say the sounds in **see**. (Signal.) *Sssēēē*. 2. Say the sounds the hard way. (Signal.) *Sss* (pause) *ēēē* (pause) *ēēē*. 3. Write the word **see**. Check children's responses.

TASK 2 Children write barn, bill, pill

a. You're going to write the word (pause) **barn**. Say the sounds you write for (pause) **barn**. Get ready. Signal for each sound as the children say *b* (pause) *aaa* (pause) *rrr* (pause) *nnn*. The children are to pause two seconds between the sounds. Repeat until firm.

b. Everybody, write the word (pause) **barn**. Check children's responses.

c. Now you're going to write the word (pause) **bill**. Say the sounds you write for (pause) **bill**. Get ready. Signal for each sound as the children say *b* (pause) *iii* (pause) *lll* (pause) *lll*. The children are to pause two seconds between the sounds. Repeat until firm.

d. Everybody, write the word (pause) **bill**. Check children's responses.

e. Next you're going to write the word (pause) **pill**. Say the sounds you write for (pause) **pill**. Get ready. Signal for each sound as the children say *p* (pause) *iii* (pause) *lll* (pause) *lll*. The children are to pause two seconds between the sounds. Repeat until firm.

f. Everybody, write the word (pause) **pill**. Check children's responses.

TASK 3 Children write it

You're going to write the word **it**. Think about the sounds in (pause) **it** and write the word. Check children's responses.

TASK 4 Children write pit

a. You're going to write the word **pit**. Listen. **Pit**. Saying the sounds in (pause) **pit** the hard way. Get ready. Signal for each sound as the children say *p* (pause) *iii* (pause) *t*. The children are to pause two seconds between the sounds. Repeat until firm.

b. Everybody, write the word (pause) **pit**. Check children's responses.

SENTENCE WRITING

TASK 5 Children write a sentence

a. Listen to this sentence. **We will win a car**. Your turn. Say that sentence. Get ready. (Signal.) *We will win a car*.

b. Now you're going to say it the slow way. Get ready. Signal for each word as the children say *we* (pause) *will* (pause) *win* (pause) *a* (pause) *car*. Repeat until firm.

c. Everybody, write the sentence. Spell each word the right way. Check children's responses.

END OF SPELLING LESSON

Spelling Lesson 110

WORD WRITING

TASK 1   Children write **bar**, **pill**, **will**

a. You're going to write the word (pause) **bar**. Say the sounds you write for (pause) **bar**. Get ready. Signal for each sound as the children say *b* (pause) *aaa* (pause) *rrr*. The children are to pause two seconds between the sounds. Repeat until firm.

b. Everybody, write the word (pause) **bar**. Check children's responses.

c. Now you're going to write the word (pause) **pill**. Say the sounds you write for (pause) **pill**. Get ready. Signal for each sound as the children say *p* (pause) *iii* (pause) *lll* (pause) *lll*. The children are to pause two seconds between the sounds. Repeat until firm.

d. Everybody, write the word (pause) **pill**. Check children's responses.

e. Next you're going to write the word (pause) **will**. Say the sounds you write for (pause) **will**. Get ready. Signal for each sound as the children say *www* (pause) *iii* (pause) *lll* (pause) *lll*. The children are to pause two seconds between the sounds. Repeat until firm.

f. Everybody, write the word (pause) **will**. Check children's responses.

TASK 2   Children write **ham**, **bit**, **land**

a. You're going to write the word **ham**. Think about the sounds in (pause) **ham** and write the word. Check children's responses.

To correct	1. Say the sounds in **ham**. (Signal.) *Haaammm.* 2. Say the sounds the hard way. (Signal.) *H* (pause) *aaa* (pause) *mmm.* 3. Write the word **ham**. Check children's responses.

b. Repeat *a* for **bit** and **land**.

SENTENCE WRITING

TASK 3   Children write a sentence

a. Listen to this sentence. **He had mud on him**. Your turn. Say that sentence. Get ready. (Signal.) *He had mud on him.*
b. Now you're going to say it the slow way. Get ready. Signal for each word as the children say *he* (pause) *had* (pause) *mud* (pause) *on* (pause) *him.* Repeat until firm.
c. Everybody, write the sentence. Spell each word the right way.
Check children's responses.

END OF SPELLING LESSON

Spelling Lesson 111

WORD WRITING

TASK 1   Children write **but**

You're going to write the word **but**. Think about the sounds in (pause) **but** and write the word. Check children's responses.

To correct	1. Say the sounds in **but**. (Signal.) *Buuut.* 2. Say the sounds the hard way. (Signal.) *B* (pause) *uuu* (pause) *t.* 3. Write the word **but**. Check children's responses.

TASK 2   Children write **bar**

a. You're going to write the word (pause) **bar**. Say the sounds you write for (pause) **bar**. Get ready. Signal for each sound as the children say *b* (pause) *aaa* (pause) *rrr*. The children are to pause two seconds between the sounds. Repeat until firm.
b. Everybody, write the word (pause) **bar**. Check children's responses.

TASK 3 Children write **his**, **see**, **barn**, **and**

a. You're going to write the word **his**. Think about the sounds in (pause) **his** and write the word. Check children's responses.

To correct	1. Say the sounds the hard way. (Signal.) *H* (pause) *iii* (pause) *sss*.
	2. Write the word **his**. Check children's responses.

b. You're going to write the word **see**. Think about the sounds in (pause) **see** and write the word. Check children's responses.

To correct	1. Say the sounds in **see**. (Signal.) *Sssēēē*.
	2. Say the sounds the hard way. (Signal.) *Sss* (pause) *ēēē* (pause) *ēēē*.
	3. Write the word **see**. Check children's responses.

c. Repeat *b* for **barn** and **and**.

SENTENCE WRITING

TASK 4 Children write a sentence

a. Listen to this sentence. **We are on the farm.** Your turn. Say that sentence. Get ready. (Signal.) *We are on the farm.*

b. Now you're going to say it the slow way. Get ready. Signal for each word as the children say *we* (pause) *are* (pause) *on* (pause) *the* (pause) *farm*. Repeat until firm.

c. Everybody, write the sentence. Spell each word the right way. Check children's responses.

END OF SPELLING LESSON